Opening Doors

Opening Doors

Angela Preston

authorHOUSE®

AuthorHouse™ UK
1663 Liberty Drive
Bloomington, IN 47403 USA
www.authorhouse.co.uk
Phone: 0800.197.4150

Published by AuthorHouse 07/27/2015

ISBN: 978-1-5049-4570-7 (sc)
ISBN: 978-1-5049-4571-4 (hc)
ISBN: 978-1-5049-4572-1 (e)

Acknowledgements

I would like to acknowledge my wonderful parents for giving me life and a life I truly cherish, for the upbringing they provided. What we missed out on in luxuries, they more than made up for in other ways: my mum's passion for life, the laughter, joy, and love for her girls that she carried right throughout her life, and my dad's determination, loyalty, pride, and strength he instilled in his six girls. I took so much from these two people who made me what I am today.

My sisters are my five best friends. They made me laugh and cry, both sad and happy tears, growing up. The bond that our mum had woven so tightly, it would never be broken. Even to this day, we may not always agree, as we are all opinionated, independent individuals, but we are still best friends.

My beautiful nieces and nephews, as well as our precious great-grandchildren, are like my own children and have brought me so much joy over the years. My beautiful goddaughter Mollie for being the daughter I never had.

My wonderful aunty Mary, who always had her door open when we needed her. I loved her so much. My uncle Michael, who I also adored so much; he was like God to me: there when we needed him, along with my uncle John and uncle Joe.

Tracey Birch, for being my first friend and still my friend forty-two years later; her aunty Debbie, who I had my first drink and my first date with Barry along with her mum Ellen, who also played a big part in my childhood; Joan and Tony Birch for showing me empathy and treating me like one of their own.

Maxine, Lorraine, Debbie, Marie, Paula, Sandra, Mandy, Shelley, and Lynn are my friends who have had a huge impact on my life.

Colleagues and managers who have inspired me so much throughout my career.

My first manager when I was an agent, his words inspired me to become an area manager.

The human resources manager who guided me throughout my journey as an area manager.

The regional manager who believed in me and put me as interim in South Liverpool. I also have to thank him for teaching me the importance of being professional and how to become business minded.

The divisional manager who gave me the chance to shine and be successful; he gave me my very first branch. He was the one divisional manager I had aspired to be. I will always be so grateful to him.

The motivational speaker I had the pleasure of meeting, he helped me realise what my vocation was

My mentor and friend, who taught me what being a great mentor stood for.

Most importantly, my husband and sons, who are the reason my world goes around every day. Barry has never once gone against a decision I have made; his support and guidance, even what to write in my book, has been so important throughout our twenty-eight years together. His intelligence amazes me every day, as well as the love he displays for me at any opportunity. Thanks, Ba, I love you so much.

My Christopher, my Leighton, and my Joseph, my most treasured possessions. I want to thank them for making my life complete and helping me become a mum I could only have dreamt of becoming, as well as a friend.

I thank God every day I get to spend with you three, making me proud of the men you have all become. The love and respect you all show not just your dad and me as well as each other, anyone you meet, makes my heart swell with pride. You really are my everything.

Introduction

In May 2014, I quit the job that had run through my veins for so long and that I loved so much. Up until a few months before, I still woke up every day thankful I had landed this role, which I had wanted more than anything.

I had worked my way up from the grass roots and knew the ins and outs of the job. This knowledge is what led to my success.

I wanted to succeed and be effective not just for myself but also for the divisional manager, who had believed in me and given me my chance.

My work ethic was instilled in me when I was a little girl. I came from a family of six girls, four of whom were older than me. They along with our parents had shown me the importance of working hard and what you can achieve from doing this, but my hunger to succeed also started at an early age. From as far back as I can remember, I didn't take losing very well, so more often than not I studied and practiced every game we played, giving me that edge all the time, ensuring I won most of the time, and this still continues today.

I have this habit of when I do something for a second time, it has to be quicker than the first time, constantly improving.

I had been thinking about leaving my job for a long time. The year before, I had been off ill (looking back now, it was probably from sheer exhaustion). Senior management need not have put pressure on me to succeed. I did this quite well myself.

I was so ill at one point, my doctor wanted to admit me to hospital. He relented only after I promised that I would rest as well as take time off work. This was now a wakeup call for me. I had to think of my own health and my future.

Some days, I was working up to fifteen hours just to ensure results were coming in. These hours were necessary if I was to be the best I could be. If I left the office early, I felt in my mind I would fail. I continually looked for ways to improve; that's when I realised it was time to move on, plus my passion for the job was now waning.

If I got four hours of sleep a night, I was lucky, as my mind was unable to rest. I worried about taking my location to the top, so sleep deprivation played a major part in my time off.

As well as it affecting my health, it was also having a big effect on my family; first and foremost before my job, I was a mum and a wife. As much as my job was important to me, my family meant more, and wanting to be part of my boys' future was the deciding factor in my decision to leave.

It was September 2012 when my health started to deteriorate, and that is when I stopped enjoying my job. It had played such a big part in my life and had given me a good lifestyle. The job enabled me to afford luxuries for my children, and I almost couldn't believe I was contemplating leaving.

My personality began to change. I had always been known for my vivacious personality, and humour was a big part of my life. A smile was forever painted on my face, even in tough times, but right now I couldn't find anything to smile about. I was starting to become quite a negative person, which didn't suit me. When I was a little girl, my sister Marie used to say that my smile lit up my face; well, it didn't right now.

When my territory included Blackburn and Manchester, my day started at 7.30 a.m. and I often did not finish until 10.00 p.m. I missed family times and meals. I also missed talking as a family about our day. This was something I had always looked forward to before I started working such silly hours.

I have always been a hands-on mum, so missing these special moments took a toll on me.

When I got home, the boys were either in their rooms or out with friends, and I would be so tired that I didn't even bother having dinner. I would just go straight to bed after getting a quick shower. My weekends were also affected; if I wasn't on the laptop, I was sleeping. My social time was becoming part of my work life; you know the saying, 'Work to live'. I was actually living to work. I knew it was only a matter time before I made the decision.

The guilt I was feeling had overtaken what my salary afforded. It also affected my marriage. My husband, Barry, could see how tired I was. We had always spent Sundays together. They had always been our day, but that was now a thing of the past. I had always prided myself on my job as a mum and enjoyed my relationship with my sons. I learnt from my own beautiful mum that no matter what you achieve in life, your role as a mum is the most important one. This was now being compromised, so it was time to take action. The effect this would have on me personally was nothing compared to what was happening to my health and my family.

It wasn't a decision I was taking lightly. I still couldn't believe I had been given this job. I still woke up every day thanking God for my blessings. As a child, I didn't think I would achieve much, so to be doing a job I loved meant the world to me.

I worked under a lot of fantastic leaders and learned so much from them, and I led some of the most hard-working, driven, and honest managers and agents. These were the ones I would miss along with the customers. I was not only a hands-on mum, I was also a hands-on leader and manager. My greatest pleasure was to help nurture and coach others to exceed their own expectations.

I loved to watch someone grow on a daily basis; it was quite hard to now be thinking of leaving all this behind, but life goes on for everyone. I also knew that these same individuals would carry on regardless. It was time to put me first. I had also made great friends with the other area managers. Again, it would be a great wrench to leave them behind. Over the years, I had learned so much from just watching them. When I first became an area manager, I had the best mentor; he not only taught me the job but also became a great friend.

I have always been grateful to the company for my salary. This was another reason I worked so hard. I believe you should always give an honest day's work for an honest day's pay, and I always made sure I went over and beyond in my role to show my appreciation. This is what benefitted my boys and gave them the opportunities that most kids can only dream of. All three of my boys were lucky enough to work in America in summer camps in between studying. This opened doors for them that otherwise wouldn't have happened without my salary.

My husband and I made sure everything we earned went into our boys' futures; we wanted to give them the best start in life. That was what I worked so hard for: to give my boys the opportunity I promised myself I would do all those years ago.

I saw my mum and dad struggle because they couldn't provide much for us. Even though we hadn't grown up with material things, we had the best foundation of love that we would all build on throughout life. We had a bond that was woven so tightly by our mum and is still as strong today as it was all those years ago. So as much as I wanted them to experience all of the finer things in life, I also wanted them to be part of a loving, compassionate family who would always be there for each other, just like I have with my sisters, which could have been damaged if I had carried on doing my job.

I knew I was making the biggest decision of my life and that could either make or break me. I also knew my time at the company was done. I had to put both my health and my family first.

As I am sitting here writing the start of this book, my resignation has gone in, and not once have I regretted my decision. When I was twenty-eight, I had applied and been accepted to complete a course in journalism. I had to turn it down, as I couldn't afford to give up my job, having a young family at the time. So here I was in a very different place: My children, now men, and my husband supporting my decision. He told me that I can't put a price on my health as well as peace of mind.

Even the economic climate at the time didn't put me off. I know my capabilities and will always succeed, whether I am a cleaner or director of a company. I will always apply that same work ethic I have always displayed. There is a fire inside me that keeps growing and pushes me on.

Others thought I was having a midlife crisis, leaving my job to write a book and take my career in a completely different direction. I have always believed you will never know how good you are unless you leave your comfort zone.

I was excited at the thought of starting a brand-new chapter in my life. My husband and I had raised our children to be fine young men, and now it was my time.

It was also important for me to teach my children to have a good work ethic but never settle for a situation they are unhappy with. It is okay to change, as this helps us grow as individuals.

I also wanted to be the best role model to my children and ensure everything I did it would benefit them. Writing this book and taking a completely new career path was another lesson for my boys.

After I resigned, members of my family were commenting how my old personality was coming back, and by now I knew I only had three months left, and I would be starting pastures new.

I gave my notice on May 8. My husband, Barry, had booked a two-week holiday to Egypt for June, my two youngest sons were working in America for the summer, and my eldest son lived in London. A holiday would be good for both of us and also give me time to think about my future.

Only a couple of days into the holiday, Barry remarked on how he could see the peace coming back into my face, and it was here I decided to write a book about growing up in the '70s and '80s in Liverpool with the Tory government and Margaret Thatcher in office.

Life had been tough; we didn't have a lot, but most families I grew up with were similar. Some were well off, and as a little girl growing up in Radcliffe, I decided my children would have a start in life that I hadn't. As much as I would have loved the things other kids had, I was lucky to be part of a family who were always looking out for each other.

The foundation of love my mum built for us was tempered by a strict upbringing from my dad. With his army background, he ruled with an iron fist. I would not swap that upbringing for a million pounds. I believe it has helped shape me into the person I am today, as well as define me as a parent to my three boys.

I have built that same loving foundation that came from our mum to the firm and disciplined upbringing from our dad, adding compassion and empathy for each other as well as people we meet throughout our lives.

I am sure that wherever our mum and dad are today, they would be as equally proud of their six girls as Barry and I are of our boys. They have grown into men I am proud to call mine.

When I do eventually look back over the years, I will never regret my decision to leave the job I had worked so hard for and the company I had loved. It not only gave me security but also helped me grow as a person and gave me beautiful memories and friends to last a lifetime.

I am grateful that leaving has enabled me to get back precious time with my family and also play a part in my boys' futures.

Chapter 1

I grew up in a family of six girls; times were hard, but we had each other and could go without most things, as long as we were together.

What we went without in material things we more than made up for with the games we invented to keep us occupied. There were so many, we were never lonely and always had a friend in one and other.

I was the second youngest and had four older siblings to look out for me. Kathy was the eldest, then Paula, Marie, and Tricia. After me, Michelle was the baby (I still call her Bab today).

Life for the Riley family started on the third floor of the Four Squares, a tenement block; neighbours were like family, so much so that one neighbour, Winnie Burton, became my godmother.

I wouldn't know that woman if I fell over her now, but everyone else in her family was fed up with being a godmother to one of my mum's girls. I think they all must have refused the job. Even my mum was by now fed up of buying pink, so much so she left me in the nursery for days in Mill Road. It was only when my nin came to visit and asked where I was that she admitted what she had done. Her reaction was, 'I should have left you there all those years ago'. It was only then that my mum realised what she had done, and that's when the bond between us was formed so strong that nothing in this world could ever break it, not even death.

My sisters still laugh about me being the only one left in the nursery. She must have known even then how much I would talk and thought of the peace lost in the future when, above all the other five voices, mine would be the loudest.

It was normal to grow up in big families in those days. My dad had come from a family of nine (four girls and five boys); he was the second eldest and grew up in Kensington Street. My mum came from a family of eight (she was in the middle of four boys and four girls), so my mum and dad expected to have a large family.

Mum would often tell us stories of growing up in Gerard Gardens and friendships she formed from a little girl. Her smile would light up her face whenever she spoke of her childhood, a place where she felt safe and part of one of the best communities of her generation. Gerard Gardens and Gerard Crescent were still there as we were growing up, and we would go there every Wednesday to Aunty Lizzie's, Mum's cousin.

She had a big family; there was always a cup of tea at the ready for anyone who called, no matter how many were already there.

I looked forward to this so much; we would be going up the stairs and could hear the laughter coming from there. The type of community spirit found in Gerard Gardens was rare. I knew why it held such fond memories in my mum's heart.

From a young age, I knew times were tough for us. We sometimes had the bare minimum of food, but not once did we ever go without. Even if it was egg and chips, we always ate, through all those tough times. What we never lost was our spirit. There was never any spare money for luxuries or things that kids get so freely today. The spirit our mum carried right throughout her life was instilled in each one of us from an early age, and with this we could face anything. Our childhood may have been hard, but nowhere near as hard as it had been for our parents.

My mum and dad had met on a blind date, and their first real home after getting married (they lived in my nana's front room for a while) was a one-room flat in Kensington, so a three-bedroom flat in a tenement block was probably like the Ritz to them.

As young as I was, I remember thinking I would never struggle with my own children, I would make sure their start in life was not going to be as tough as mine had. Sometimes, I could see the desperation in my mum's eyes worrying where the next meal would be coming from; just looking at her would upset me.

In those days, it was the men who had jobs. My dad worked on the demolition (otherwise known as demo) from when he left the army. He started as a can lad and continued this until he retired.

As time went on, Barry and my brother in law also worked there with him.

One day, he was teaching Barry what to do; he told him there was a right way and wrong way of doing it. After they demolished the first floor and got closer to the ground, my dad told him to stop for a minute and look up. There was a loose brick at the top of the building. His words to Barry were, 'See that brick? It is very important, and when we finish, remind me, and I will tell you why'.

Later on, in the wagon on the way home, Barry asked the importance of this brick. My dad replied, 'If that brick had fallen on your head, you would have ended up soft and given all your money to our Angela'. That was my dad's dry sense of humour. Another time, he was moaning at Barry about the time he was taking coming back with an empty wheel barrow. Barry said, 'It's not easy pushing it, Eddie', as it was usually overloaded and hard to push up the plank into the skip. Again, his sarcastic reply was, 'I know, because if it was easy, I would be doing it myself'.

Barry often commented on how brilliant his mind was and how good he was at problem solving. He would go down on one knee as he pondered the job in front of him and then determine what materials to get. He said at the time he often thought it wouldn't work, but sure enough, it worked every time.

It was unreal how much knowledge he accumulated over the years. This is where I must have got my problem solving from, as I would be doing the same years later in my role.

Mum at the time would stay at home to look after the kids and house, so with one wage and six kids to look after, life was always going to be a struggle.

I look back on those times and see this has defined the person I have become. If someone asked me would I swop those times, my answer would always be no. As hard as it was, I had the most loving mum anyone could wish for and five sisters who are still my best friends today; even if we have disagreements, we are always there for each other. This is the reason for writing this book.

No matter where you come from or what your upbringing, the sky is the limit if you push yourself. The desire to succeed as well as inspire others is in us all; it depends on whether you want it enough. The struggles we had growing up pushed me on to always grow as a person, as well as motivated me to help others believe in themselves and want to achieve more. I believe whatever you get out of life, you should always put back by teaching others.

Chapter 2

Around my fifth birthday, we moved to a house with a garden; the rent was £7 per week. I still remember the excitement in my mum and dad's faces when we arrived in our new home in Radcliffe Walk. It seemed huge at the time; we had been used to having everything on one floor, so we were running up and down the stairs like kids possessed. You can just imagine the noise. No carpets on the stairs, a brand-new house. The noise would echo all over, my dad screaming at the top of his voice to keep the noise down and my mum still so excited at getting her own home.

Mum carried this joy and wonder right throughout her life, always with the biggest, most beautiful smile spread across her face.

By now, Kathy was twelve and clothes were usually handed down once they went too small on the older ones. We had three bedrooms, Mum and Dad in one, Kathy in another, and the rest of us were in the third bedroom.

As we got older, we would laugh at how it was like Colomendy, a place in Wales where we would go with the school for five days. I couldn't wait to get there, as everyone had spoken about the fun you had. One of the dormitories was meant to be haunted by a man called Peg Leg. Everyone was terrified of being put there.

I'll never forget how I had been banned from swimming; I had a fight with a girl from another school, who had picked a fight with one of my friends, who was quiet. As young as I was, I still stood up for what I believed in. I have never liked bullies.

I felt it was my duty to stand up and take on the girl. My punishment for fighting was to stand in the swimming baths and watch everyone else swim, even though I thought at the time I was doing good. That should have taught me then to keep quiet. Needless to say, today I am still that same person, even if it does get me into trouble.

In our bedroom, we had a row of three beds, Paula in her own, I shared with Marie, and Michelle and Tricia shared. If we wanted more space, we doubled them up as bunk beds. That gave us the space to play. In those days, we had toy fights. Where we grew up, you had to be tough. Marie and Paula taught me from an early age how to stand up for myself. Kathy, Tricia, and Michelle were the quiet ones. If I needed someone to look out for me, it was always Paula and Marie I went to.

It was in that bed from a little girl that the bond between Marie and myself was built; it is still as strong today. Although we are all very close as sisters, Marie and I have always gone on holiday together, with our husbands. The memories we have made over the years are quite different from what the rest of us have.

Marie would buy comics called *Mandy*, *Bunty*, and *Judy*. The two of us would get lost in them for hours, sometimes pretending we were part of the stories.

There were two stories I looked forward to every week: *The Four Marys* (their full names were Mary Field, Mary Cotter, Mary Radley, and Mary Simpson; they were in a boarding school and their beds were in a row just like ours, so I could relate to them) and *The Guardian Tree*. The character in this story was called Rose, and she would go to the tree when she needed guidance or advice. This tree reminded me of our mum. She guarded each of us with her life.

We really were her most treasured possessions. She had this knack for making every one of us feel number one in her heart. We also believed that anything was possible if you wanted it enough. This is a trait I have taken on as a mum to my own boys today.

When growing up, the older ones were helping around the house. This allowed my mum to take a cleaning job in the university. She would leave the house by 5.30.

This is where Kathy would eventually do part of her teacher training, years later. It is strange that some of those rooms my mum cleaned, my sister would be learning the ropes of becoming a teacher in.

Our parents instilled different qualities within each of us: my mum's passion and enthusiasm for life and the love for her children, along with my dad's determination, strong will, loyalty, and pride in everything he done. He wore a suit and cap everywhere he went. These were values that all six of us still carry through life today, and the same qualities are in all the grandchildren.

Chapter 3

Life was still tough for us; yes, we may have had a house with a garden, and there was now two wages coming in, but there were still the usual bills to pay.

There was now the new crazes that were out. Whether it was clothes or gadgets, we could still not afford them, although there were kids I grew up with who did have the latest thing. I never once envied these kids. I accepted what we had was far more than money could buy. The six of us knew what the other was thinking and could relate to each other better than anyone.

What this did for me was to make me dream big and want to make something of myself years later for my own family. Though money was tight and we missed out on material things, what we learned from our parents would help us grow and succeed as adults.

Within a few years of us moving to Radcliffe Walk, our eldest sister became pregnant at sixteen, which at the time you would have thought she committed a murder because of the shame felt by my dad. He was very old fashioned and saw this as an embarrassment, not realising she wasn't the only one at the time of her generation to fall pregnant at a young age.

This would affect the rest of us and how we were allowed to live our lives as young girls. Looking back, I can understand my dad. At the time, his pride was dented, and he was hurt.

Kathy went on to have a daughter, Dominique, and she became the centre of my dad's universe. She brought so much love and joy into our lives. My dad's anger soon disappeared.

Being ten at the time, I remember wondering why he had been so angry. I didn't really understand; All he was thinking about was my sister's future and the influence it could have had on the rest of us.

Dominique brought so much happiness that she became the seventh daughter, and still to this day, she is known as the aunty cousin to all her cousins; she lived with us until she was eight.

From a young age and growing up, it was normal for parents to argue. There was always something going on in a big family where arguments came naturally. Mine seemed to get worse at the time of Kathy's pregnancy, due to laying the blame with each other.

I walked in one summer afternoon and saw my dad arguing with mum. I thought, *This has got to stop*, being so young and not realising this was a normal marriage.

That afternoon, I decided this should stop once and for all and called on my friend Tracey Birch. I didn't tell her where we were going, I just asked her would she come with me to town. Off we went to Stanley Street in Liverpool town centre, to a divorce lawyer called Malcom J Ross.

I had heard his advertisements on the radio from when I would sit in the kitchen with my mum. Looking back, you wonder how marriages did last so long then. The only time they seemed to talk was to argue. My mum sat in the kitchen, listening to the radio, all day. She often took part in the competitions with Billy and Wally in 'Hold Your Plums', as well as listen to Pete Price and little Billy Marr. If you went into the kitchen and Billy and Wally were on, you couldn't talk. If you did, Mum would scream the place down and tell you to go out. My dad sat in the living room, reading *The Echo*. It was so big, all you could see were his legs. The chippy would cut these into four pieces to wrap the fish and chips in.

This man was said to be the best divorce lawyer in Liverpool, according to the radio, so it was only natural to go there; also, I hadn't heard of any others at the time.

When we arrived, Tracey asked why we were there, and I told her I was making an appointment for my mum to get a divorce. Her reaction was, 'What?'

I said, 'Well, all they seem to do is argue, and I think it would be easier if my dad wasn't there'.

It wasn't like her house, nice and peaceful; at the time. It was just her mum and dad, Tracey and her brother Tony (Kate came along a few years later). Whenever I went there as a child, their home was filled with so much love and happiness, that I foolishly thought if my dad was gone, our house would be the same.

He ruled our house with an iron fist; since Kathy had Dominique, we would tiptoe around the house if my dad was in bed. If we made a noise, he would bang down to keep it down. I saw this as controlling, not really thinking of the hours he had been working. Getting enough sleep was something that was necessary, not just because it was physical work but also the danger that came with it if he didn't think on his feet when completing this job. He had to always be aware of his surroundings, and not getting the proper sleep could have had a huge impact on him and his colleagues.

I was determined to get this appointment, and no one was going to stop me, even Tracey trying to get me to change my mind. As young as she was, she knew this was normal in all families. Well, I wouldn't listen and decided, 'I am here now, I might as well speak to someone'. Again, that stubbornness showing itself in me, even as young as ten.

I went to the counter. I remember being so small that I couldn't even see over it. The lady had to lean over, as she couldn't see me. She asked if she could help, and I said, 'Yes, I would like to make an appointment with Malcolm J Ross for my mum to get a divorce please'.

She just looked at me and laughed.

I remember thinking, *Who is she laughing at? I am serious.* Here was this smartly dressed lady in her pencil skirt and black court shoes. What did she know? What gave her the right to laugh? Looking back, she was probably laughing at this little person who even on tiptoes still couldn't see over the counter.

Through my determination and steeliness, she finally brought Malcolm J Ross out. I explained why I was there; he didn't laugh or look at me with sadness, but with sheer amazement that this kid as little as I was and being so young had still somehow found her way to his office.

I remember him asking how I had heard about him. I told him it was from the radio advertisement. He was exactly how I would have pictured him: dark curly hair, grey pinstriped suit, and a pink shirt and tie. Years later, when I told this story to Barry, he told me his mum worked in the restaurant across the path from his office, and she would cook his favourite meal of steak and kidney pudding; in the summer holidays he would deliver it to him.

Mr Ross sat me down and asked me why I wanted to see my mum and dad divorced. I told him the story of Kathy's pregnancy and all the rows between my parents, as well as how happy I thought Tracey's house was.

He looked at me and asked my name. I told him, and his words to me were, 'Angela, all mums and dads argue; it doesn't mean they should get divorced. Go home and tell them how you feel. You may be surprised by their reaction. What I will do is give you my card, and if your mum decides she needs advice, she can contact me'.

Even though he thought it quite amusing, he still displayed empathy towards me, trying to make me realise this was normal in households with large families, especially those with not much spare cash. I remember thinking years later how that man came down to my level of being a child and used the lingo that I would understand.

I thought I was great at the time, all grown up, going on the bus into town. I thought, *I'll show him*. I returned home with a smile plastered across my face and the card in my pocket.

I walked up to the front door, thinking if I heard my dad's voice shouting, I'd just give this card straight to my mum. When I went in, it was all quiet, no arguing, mum as usual in the kitchen listening to the radio, and my dad in the living room. Well, I wasn't expecting this; the smile went away and out came the card from my pocket. I was playing with it in my hand as my mum walked past and asked what it was. I wished later I hadn't told her, after the reaction I got. I just came out with it as though it was normal for a ten-year-old to go and see a divorce lawyer. When you think of today, kids can actually divorce their parents. Probably just as well parents couldn't divorce theirs. At the time, mine would have, without looking back.

I started with, 'Well, Mum, I just thought you would be better off if you got a divorce. I thought I would get the card for you, and if Dad argues with you again, you can ring him up'.

Wasn't I in for a shock, by the reaction I got?

'You've what?' she said; she was like a lunatic, not only telling their private business to a stranger, but going into town on a bus and crossing roads. I forgot about that; how naïve of me. I never thought that through.

I said, 'But Mum, he's lovely; he'll help you'. As I was saying this, she tried to grab hold of me to give me a belt. I was too quick and legged it up the stairs. She was still screaming at the top of her voice, 'Eddie, you'll never believe what she has done'.

I now knew it was serious. She never, ever told my dad anything we did, nor had she ever hit me before.

This was the only time I can remember getting hit from her; my dad, on the other hand, was the one who disciplined us, and she knew how strict he was. Here I was, waiting for what would probably be a good hiding, which was what you got in them days, thinking I had done her a favour.

With all the noise, he came running out of the living room to find out what was going on. When she told him, he burst out laughing and thought it was hilarious.

Here I was, the second youngest of six, with the audacity to try and split them up. All he kept saying was, 'We have been married nearly twenty years, and you're trying to get us divorced', and my mum in the background saying, 'I love your father'.

Well, even my dad was surprised by that, never mind me. He didn't do what I expected; he just didn't speak to me, which was probably worse than getting a hiding (at least that was over within seconds).

Looking back, what a lesson I got that day. Here I was, thinking the best thing for all of us would be for my mum and dad to divorce, and they displayed that solidarity that only married couples show. Through all the difficult times in their lives, as well the arguments between them, they would still be together right up until my beloved mum's death, after forty-four years, never spending an anniversary apart. He made sure even death would not let that happen.

It was the joke for years with my parents and sisters at what I had done. Even as young as ten, I demonstrated that stubbornness and objectivity that is still in me today.

Chapter 4

As much as there were hard times where money and luxuries were concerned, there were also many great times.

Sundays were my favourite day. I would get lost in *Black Beauty* and waited with baited breath for this to come on at tea time. For a while, we couldn't afford a TV after it had broken, but when Paula got older and started working, she bought one. At the time, it cost £18; imagine that today you couldn't even get a toy one. It was only black-and-white, but we were delighted with it.

More *Black Beauty* for me to watch, even if everything was the same colour. Saturday nights were the same, watching the day's highlights from the Liverpool match. I was never able to watch them live, as I am too nervous watching them and dread them getting beaten. My poor husband still has to turn over if the other team scores against them.

That passion for football didn't come from my dad; would you believe it, my mum adored them. All her brothers were Everton supporters, but she loved her beloved Liverpool, and like her, it ran through the veins of five of her girls. Our eldest sister and my dad were Evertonians.

Being from Liverpool, it was only natural to support one or the other; another reason to argue, mainly my mum this time, through her passion for the Reds. We still laugh today. She had Bill Shankly on the wall for years.

She didn't even have us nor my dad on the wall. My dad would joke how he had pride of place in the living room. When they played, she would take him down and place him on the TV, and if they won, she was convinced this was the reason why (if she forgot to do it and they got beaten, there was hell to pay). My poor dad got a dog's life, but he laughed about it.

This is also where my passion for football came from. When I was a child, watching the highlights on match of the day, I would say I was going to walk down the aisle to tune away from it. Terry McDermott was my favourite player. As I got older and Ronnie Whelan started playing, I loved him even more, and then came Kenny Dalglish. Well, he was the king from the word go.

My mum's love would shine through when she spoke of one of her girls or grandchildren, but even more so for her beloved Liverpool. I still have Bill Shankly on my bedroom wall, as a testament to my precious girl.

The funniest thing about it all, my dad let slip years later: she didn't even know where Anfield was, even though the Reds played only a ten-minute bus ride away.

Imagine her delight when years later, my nephew James would play in a five-a-side tournament at Anfield. He was very determined to play, although he had broken a bone in his leg. He was that strong-minded that he played anyway. We all tried to talk him out of it, but he was adamant. You don't get many chances to play there, and the determination my dad had instilled in his girls was just as strong in his grandchildren.

Off we all went to the ground to support him. You could see the pain in his face, but he wouldn't give up and played on. You would think he was in the first team, the way we carried on, but that memory of playing at the ground he was brought up to adore will stay with him forever.

Her adoration for her team continued right up until she died. *You'll Never Walk Alone* was played as they carried her body into the church; it was also written on her headstone. The whole family, including all the husbands and grandchildren, are red through and through. We still say our eldest sister changed her colours because Everton started winning with Howard Kendall. We joked she was a glory hunter. Even though my dad was cremated and his ashes are with my mum, it was only years later that I could actually put blue flowers on the grave. I felt like a turncoat, but I also know deep down she would want us to put blue on for him as well as red for her.

Chapter 5

As we grew, the older ones started working; life became easier for us. We still didn't get as much as our friends, but we were able to do more. They would contribute to the household. They would also provide for me, Tricia, and Michelle when they could.

Through the hard times of sharing meals and playing games and laughing so much our bellies hurt (you would hear the laughing from the street) to also making names up for each other. Two of the names I can still remember were Pauline Dondge and Linda Battlewheel. Marie made up those names. She would be my mum and Tricia was Michelle's. They would put on my mum's overalls that she wore for her job and pretend to go to work. Michelle and I would have to get the house ready for when they returned.

These memories always bring a tear as well as a smile when I think of them, because through those hard times, our spirits never faulted. We still laugh about them today. I Spy was another game that we played for hours on end, and hot and cold; this was a game where you would hide something, and if the other person was getting closer, they would be warm. If they moved away from it, this was cold, and when they were stood right by it, we would say this is hot. These games would keep us occupied for hours. Imagine kids today playing games like that.

As I said, Sundays were my favourite day, because as well as watching *Black Beauty*, my mum and dad would go out and bring back tripe, pigs feet, and pigs bellies. When I think of what I ate as a child, it turns my stomach, although we were never ill. Our dad used to say we had stomachs made of steel. Pans of scouse and pea soup were cheap meals but really tasty and filling as well as warm on a cold night.

We would play these games along with pretending to shop. We would take all the food from the cupboards. I never wanted Marie to grow up, and I made the most of every minute with her.

Chapter 6

Like me, my mum mustn't have been very good at counting. A Fray Bentos pie was shared between eight of us, full half to my dad and the other half between the rest of us. No wonder I love the corners of pies; this must have been the parts I got. Even when I had my own kids, my dad still saved the corners for me. The first meal my mum cooked for him was a Fray Bentos, and she tried to pass it off as making it herself. She would have got away with it if she had been a bit more clever; he found the tin in the bin.

Every Sunday, we also had salt fish, but really it wasn't salt fish. My dad got the fish, and we got the water with big dollops of Echo margarine in it. We would all sit at the table with a big plate of toast, dipping it in the water with the margarine dripping off it.

I grew up only liking the juice, as I called it, off the salt fish and was so convinced by my mum that this was the best part. When I met Barry, who is now my husband and stayed in his house one Saturday, I woke up to the smell of salt fish.

Most Liverpool homes woke up with salt fish every Sunday. I thought, *Ooh, lovely, big plate of toast with the water and margarine.* When he walked in with two plates, one with fish and the other with two pieces of bread, I looked at him and asked, 'What's that? I wanted salt fish'.

He said, 'That is', looking at me as though I was stupid.

I knew it was salt fish, but not what I normally had. Well, when I went into the kitchen and poured the water into the bowl and then put margarine in, he looked at me with even more amazement. He asked, 'What are you doing with that?'

'I only have the juice with toast dipped in', I explained.

Barry's reaction? Put it this way: just as well he hadn't eaten his fish, or he probably would have brought it back up, watching me dipping my toast into the water and eating it. He said it's a wonder my insides wasn't shrivelled up with all the salt in the water. This water would have been steeping overnight so the amount of salt in it would definitely shrivel your stomach.

Again, just like the Fray Bentos pie, my dad got the best part, because he was the man of the house. When the *Echo* got delivered, no one was allowed to read it until he had. As usual, me being the rebellious one used to wait for it to pop through the letterbox. I would take it into the toilet to read the obituaries.

I was doing this from about nine. My mum used to read them and would say, 'Oh, how heart-breaking such a one has died'.

Well, me being curious, I think this is where I learned to read. When I think back a little nine-year-old kid reading the deaths, how morbid. Again, another Liverpool thing: reading the deaths.

I never read anything else, only this page. Years later, Barry used to joke and say how everyone dies in alphabetical order.

You could have timed your watch on the paper boy; it was always delivered at quarter to five. Marie used to say, 'You're going to get caught doing that, and he'll kill you'. One night, as I went to put it back on the floor at quarter past five, my dad caught me.

It would have to be all neat when he got it; by the time it got to me, it would We all scrunched up. Well, she was right again. When I did get caught, he nearly killed me, but not for messing the pages up. I made sure I was gentle when turning the pages. I don't know what I would have done if a page had been torn, but when he found out I was reading the deaths (he only found out after hitting me on the head with it; I was screaming and saying, 'I've only read the deaths'), well, I got another belt, because the paper was now all scrunched up. I still read that page up until a few years ago; old habits die hard.

Once my own kids were old enough, they started to have salt fish. They don't like the fish like their dad. They love my mum's traditional juice with toast, so I know my mum's memory and her traditions will be around for a long time to come. Barry and I still laugh at my face that day when he came out with fish and no juice, as kids, we called it 'Eddie Riley salt fish'. My dad made a song up: 'Eddie Riley salt fish, if you don't like Eddie Riley, you don't like salt fish', and we thought it was hilarious at the time. He'd sing this song to all the grandchildren.

Through all the tough times and hardships we may have faced, there were traditions that were kept even in poor families, like the salt fish steeping overnight on a Saturday, along with a big pan of mushy peas ready for the Sunday roast. Sunday wouldn't have been the same without these traditions.

Chapter 7

Growing up with five sisters, it was never lonely: one to fight with, one to have fun with, and one who would inspire you as you grew up. If we did argue or fight as girls do, especially over clothes, we weren't allowed to fall out; my mum said, 'There were enough people outside who will want to fight with you; you must always stick together as I have brought you up', and still to this day, even if we do fall out, we are always there for each other in times of need. Again, this is another trait I have of my mum's. My boys have always been best friends, and the laughter throughout my house with them was just like when we were kids.

As the years went on and more money became available, my mum took us to a caravan in Edwards Camp in Wales. The lady who owned it worked with my mum and gave it at a cheap rate. Us Riley's had gone without so much for years, now here we were, going to Wales in a caravan.

Wales to me was like going to the other side of the world. It was only the five girls and my mum, as Kathy was living with her husband and Dominique. My dad didn't come. I think he was delighted for the peace. When I think back to the noise of seven women, including my mum, I often wonder how my poor dad didn't run away.

To this day, I will always remember how lucky we were to even get there. The only thing we done really was play with a bat and ball all day and the compendium game; we were entertained for hours. The smell of the grass and the sun shining on us all day was enough to keep us happy.

The second year we went there, we missed the train home to Liverpool, and the only way we could get back was to go to Crewe and wait around until one in the morning for the connection. I remember at the time thinking it was an adventure to be out so late.

The third year we went, my dad decided he wanted to come with us. Well, I was devastated, because I didn't think we needed him anyway. Marie tried to make the situation better, and being five years older than me, I hung on every word that came out of her mouth. I would do anything she asked. She pointed out, 'Ange, if Dad comes with us, we'll be able to do more because there will be more money available'.

A light switch came on. I remember thinking at the time, as much as I didn't want him to come, Marie was right.

I had always wanted to go on the bikes that fitted four on. 'Do you think we'll get to go on them bikes, Marie?' I asked her.

'We can only ask, Ange', was her reply.

You could hire these bikes for one hour with a fee of around £2; kids would ride around on them all day. I would stand, mesmerised, watching these kids, thinking how lucky they were to ride them and wishing that I could do the same. I never asked if we could ride one, because even as young as I was, I knew how much of a struggle it was to get us here, so that in itself we had to be grateful for. I certainly wouldn't have hurt my mum by asking for something she couldn't give us.

One year, because she had gone with such little money, we ran out quite quickly. She decided to pawn her wedding ring in a little jewellers in the town centre. She had to go back the following week to get it out. Looking back, it must have cost more in train fare alone to get it back, so riding on one of them bikes was just out of the question.

Going back to my dad coming with us, well, I was still not happy and dreading it. I remember having that horrible gut wrench feeling in my stomach at the thought of it, but I thought, *Well, everyone else was happy, and he wasn't going to change his mind, so I might as well get used to it.*

That holiday turned out to be the best holiday we ever had at Edwards' Camp. It stayed with me for many years; yes, I finally got to hire that bike I was always so desperate to ride.

Marie was right. It was a better holiday with our dad. We even went to the beach and ate fish and chips, something new. Also, my mum and dad seemed to enjoy each other's company, even if it was only for one week. No worry or problems about where the meals were coming from, just lots of laughter still playing the compendium games, from snakes and ladders to draughts, as well as Monopoly and cards, but even then, my passion for winning was evident. If I was getting beaten, I would tip the board and refuse to play.

That competiveness and will to win was there for everyone to see and is still as strong today, only I don't tip boards up anymore. I just ensure I study and take action where needed to ensure I am successful. It is also in each of my three boys, especially Christopher. Anything he puts his hand to, he has always been successful.

I remember one year, he was in a table tennis competition in a school in Liverpool with a few other kids from his school. My friend Sandra and I had taken him and her son Francis to the competition.

Whilst I was waiting for the games to start, I decided to play. Again, I had always played this game in the youth centre when I was his age, and I was quite good for a girl (so I was told at the time).

As I was playing and spinning the ball, more and more people were coming to watch me. I just saw Christopher come walking towards me with embarrassment on his face, saying, 'I knew that was you'.

As he was practising, all the kids were running up and telling him there was a woman playing, and you should see her. He was mortified at his mum spinning the ball, and Francis was asking Sandra why she couldn't play like me, so here were two kids annoyed at their mums, one because she could play, and the other because she couldn't.

Christopher still thinks it was embarrassing when we talk about it today, so as you can see, that hunger to win was born and bred in me from a little girl. I think that came with a survival instinct, because I grew up with so little.

Chapter 8

All my sisters played different parts in my life growing up, but my love for each and every one of them was immense.

Kathy being the eldest, I haven't got many childhood memories growing up with her. She was a mum herself when I was still a child, and the respect I have for her is still as strong today as it was when I would call to her house with my friends. She had nice furniture and was so pretty. I used to say she reminded me of Princess Diana, such a gentle face, just like my mum's. Kathy was also the one who inspired me to be successful. She turned heartache into something positive and went on to become a teacher at twenty-nine, so I knew I always wanted to follow in her footsteps.

When I was twelve, Kathy gave birth to Joseph. From birth, he had problems, and Kathy only twenty. She was still a child herself, and this is when Dominique came to stay with us, as Kathy had to spend more or less the full eleven months of Joseph's life in the hospital. This is where Dominique became the seventh sister. She grew up alongside us for eight years before going home.

Kathy lost Joseph just before her twenty-first birthday; the pain that came with losing him was heart-breaking. This was when I first felt real pain. I had seen my mum's brothers and sisters die and noticed the effect it had on her, but I didn't really understand. I was now nearly fourteen when we lost Joseph, and to see the pain in Kathy's eyes was horrendous. He also was our first boy after all the girls; for him to now be gone was unimaginable.

Kathy was sedated until the funeral to try and help her. Marie carried that tiny coffin, so small; that is the reason my respect just grows every day for her.

She could have gone down a very different path and been consumed by grief, but Kathy chose to go on and serve children. Now being a mum myself, I often think of what got Kathy through those dark days, but the strength and determination our dad had instilled in each of us got her through. That strength of character she displayed at the loss of Joseph was also what pushed her to become a fantastic teacher.

My son Leighton completed teacher training in the same school as part of his degree. He was in awe of what a wonderful teacher she is and how much she respects her children, which is so important if children are to blossom.

Paula was always the one who took on the role of getting us all in. We were like sheep. She would herd us all in, including my mum, and wouldn't rest until we were all in on time. She is still like this today with all the grandchildren. They all dread when they see her number on their phone, as this means they have to go home, but I always knew growing up, no matter what happened, Paula was always there for each of us.

Then there was Marie; she was my first best friend before Tracey. She would be there to give advice on everything from boys to clothes, to me getting bullied in senior school. She always had the right answer and is still my best friend today. We have a holiday together every year along with friends Lynn, Donna and Sharon.

Tricia was the mum of the six of us and would make sure the house was kept clean when my mum and dad went out to work. She made sure we were fed; her roasts were exactly like our mum's. She still keeps this Sunday tradition for anyone who wants one today.

I was the one who loved to be around them all; my love for helping others, even as a little girl, was so strong even then.

I would often go without to save my mum money, just so I knew she wasn't struggling to buy food. I would always have the cheapest clothes and shoes, so there was money left over.

I remember one year for my birthday, my mum had promised me a sovereign ring. She only promised me this to shut me up, as they really were expensive. When my birthday came around, she had paid £15 off it in a shop called Biggars in Prescot Street. The sovereign was about £85, so I knew it was out of reach.

I also knew my mum had no other money, so there was no point kicking up a fuss. If I could get her some of it back, I would. I settled for a heart-shaped signet ring that cost £9, giving my mum enough money back to pay for that night's tea.

I was heartbroken last year when I lost that ring in West Wales, after having it for thirty-four years; it had meant so much to me over the years.

I was also known by Kathy as Hans Christian Anderson. I always had a story to tell; to now be sitting here, writing a book, it is uncanny that name would play a major part in my decision to write.

I was probably always the most extroverted out of the six of us and the one always willing to take chances (some paying off and some not).

Then there was the baby of us all, Michelle, the quietest of the six of us. Although I was bullied in senior school once, I have always been able to stand up for myself, as well others less fortunate, so if anyone said one word to Michelle, they had me to deal with. She always made sure my mum and dad were well looked after, right up until their deaths. When we were kids growing up together, she always got a bit more than I did, because she was the youngest, and I saw this as her being spoilt, so on every picture she had, I would write 'Witch' on them; we still laugh about it.

I was always curious about the world and how big it was. When Paula was around eighteen, she went to Colorado with her friend for three weeks. That was like a lifetime without her, but this is when my sense of adventure started, because that's when I realised there was a big world outside Liverpool.

One time myself, Tracey, and our other friend Tooty decided we would just keep walking until we found the end of the earth. I think we only got as far as Everton Road and turned back, but my desire to reach for more was always there.

Chapter 9

Growing up, Radcliffe Walk was a place you could leave your front door open. When we were kids, everyone knew each other, and we had siblings who were also friends. It felt just like my mum had described her childhood in Gerard Gardens, a community where everyone helped each other.

It was only when drugs became big in the eighties that it actually changed. Heroin was a major problem in Liverpool when I got to my teenage years, and Radcliffe Walk was also affected by it. Even though it was usually kids like us who were vulnerable to this drug, we would never have dared to touch any sort of drug or get involved in it, as our dad was so strict. That was enough to put us off.

Radcliffe was supposedly based on a little fishing village in Cornwall. Well, I wish we would have had the beach that Cornwall has. Our nearest beach was Crosby and New Brighton.

We chose to go to New Brighton, because it didn't just have a beach. It also had a funfair, as well as an open-air baths, that was once used in the '60s to hold beauty competitions.

This was the place all the kids would go to in the summer holidays and Sundays when it was hot, not just from Radcliffe, but from all over Liverpool. Lime Street Station would be packed to the rafters with all us kids, as well as when we got there, the kids from Wirral. New Brighton was an extremely busy place. We also went to a place in Liverpool called the Buckets off Dale Street. We would go home soaking wet after climbing in as the water was being tipped from bucket to bucket.

Sundays were great days in the summer. We would start off at the water fountain in William Brown Street, then the museum and the art gallery, being nuisances and using our coats to slide along the floors, security guards running all around the building trying to get us out. This was probably the worst thing us kids done growing up. We never had any money but would be out for hours, all treading home absolutely soaked through to the skin, and the thing was, we were never sick.

From the museum, we would head to the Pier Head, where Mrs Kelly and her daughter Maureen from Radcliffe Walk would sell the most delicious doughnuts. She would give us the doughnuts for free and tell us all to be careful going home. That was the thing about Radcliffe Walk – it was huge, but everyone looked out for each other, and we all knew our own from that estate. When I think of the age I was travelling around with my friends, I must have been only ten when we would walk all the way to the Pier Head.

As well as going to New Brighton with my friends, Marie was working as a machinist, her first job, and she was earning a wage, just as Paula had before her, she would help out with money. She would also take Tricia, Michelle, and me to New Brighton.

It was a cheap day out, as the only money spent would be the train fare and the money to go into the baths. We would take a packed lunch of spam butties, crisps, and the little orange and raspberry drinks. Looking back, I took chances then, even some boys wouldn't take as well as Marie and Tricia. I would climb on the top of the biggest diving board (I think it was thirty feet) and jump off, so that sense of adventure was in me from a child. Marie didn't just take us out on a Sunday. Most Saturdays, she would take us to London Road. We would spend the day in TJ Hughes, looking at all the makeup, and then have our dinner in the café. She still does this to this day. She has gone from taking all the grandchildren out, to now doing the same with the great-grandchildren.

Marie has been the mum to all of them and gets Mother's Day presents from most of them every year. They have all been so lucky to have her in their lives.

Chapter 10

When Liverpool became the place for fashion, many new stores opened in the city.

It was Easter, and Next had just opened; it was like Debenhams today. You could only shop there if you had money. My friend Tracey and her mum were going into town, and I went with them. Tracey got a lovely green suit for Easter, along with a checked one. God, I longed for a suit like that, but I was so happy she had got it. So as not to leave me out, her mum bought me a top, which I remember thinking even then, how lovely of Joan to think of me.

I will never forget the kindness that Joan Birch had shown me. She knew we struggled as a family, and my mum would not have been able to afford to shop in Next, but she also wanted me to enjoy the happiness that Tracey had shown when getting her clothes. I decided then I would always help people less fortunate than myself when I grew up, just as Joan had done for me.

The excitement I had shown for getting that top, you could have bottled it and sold it on, there was that much. That excitement is still as strong today when I receive something. Barry says he loves to buy me presents because of the excitement I display on my face, and that comes from that top bought for me all those years ago from a lady who I still hold in high regard today.

As well as my beloved mum being my first inspiration in life, through all the trials and tribulations she had faced, not just raising six girls with very little cash, but also grieving from the losses of her brothers and sisters, who had all died in their prime, leaving children motherless or fatherless. She would still have that smile painted across her face, as well as loving arms and a shoulder when needed.

Joan Birch would go on to become another inspiration in my life, as a person who shared what she had with me. It may have only been a top to Joan, but it was everything I could have dreamt of to wear something from Next.

The following Saturday, off I went into town to get my clothes with Tracey, only I didn't go to Next. I went to a place called St John's Precinct; this was market stalls where you could get clothes and shoes at a discounted price. Because it was so cheap, I had enough money to get two skirts and one top. Well, I was thrilled. I bought a yellow skirt to match the top Joan had bought me the week before and a blue and white skirt and top for Easter Monday. I couldn't believe that I had two sets of clothes, because there was so many of us, I was lucky to get one, so to now have two, I thought it was Christmas and Easter rolled into one.

When I got home, Marie had also been to town. She would have been around nineteen, and I was around fourteen. We weren't much different in size. She had been to Next and bought a pink skirt with a pleat down the front and pockets on both sides, as well as a pink popover and a white t shirt. My eyes were like saucers when I saw them. My sister had been shopping in Next. How proud was I; she then asked what I had bought. I was so excited to have two sets, I couldn't contain my excitement. I could see the sadness in Marie's eyes. You could see by looking at them how cheap they were. I still would have worn them. My parents had worked hard to pay for them, and I was thankful for that.

Easter Sunday came; it was to be our first time in Southport with all my friends. Marie woke me up early. Southport was a million miles away for the kids of Radcliffe Walk, so we were all ecstatic to get there.

I went into the living room, and her new clothes were laid out on the settee, and she had a smile on her face.

'I've got a surprise for you', she said. 'I have decided to let you wear my new clothes I bought yesterday'.

She said she knew I was happy with the clothes I had bought, but she wanted me to wear the set she had bought. I was crying with excitement; I was thrilled to wear a top from Next, never mind the whole caboodle. Imagine little old me who would more often than not wear clothes passed down to me, to now be wearing a brand-new set from a top store.

She still says today she will never forget my reaction and the smile that would cover the whole of my face.

Chapter 11

Off I went to Southport, feeling like a princess, with all my friends and thinking I still had two sets at home. Christmas really had come early.

Well, the worst possible thing that could happen actually did: Marie had been good enough to let me have the clothes before she had the chance to wear them, so the least I could have done was look after them, but without knowing, someone had put a cigarette burn right in the front of the skirt.

Imagine the fear when I saw it. It wasn't just what she would do, but I felt like I had let her down by not taking care of her clothes. She had worked two jobs to pay for her belongings, and I had let this happen. She had shown me so much kindness to let me wear them, so I decided I wasn't going home.

When we got back to Radcliffe Walk at five o'clock that night, all my friends had gone in, and I was just walking around for what felt like hours.

On the estate there were covers, the bedrooms of the houses that you could shelter under when it was raining. I decided to sit here for a while, thinking of where I was going to go. I was sitting there and could hear Paula shouting my name at the top of her voice. I knew she would be panicking because I had been with her once before when Tricia had stayed out late. I also knew she was only happy when she knew we were all in. The fear and hurt I caused to Marie was stronger than the urge to answer her calls.

It was around seven thirty, and it was getting quite chilly. My legs were getting cold so I pulled my legs up to my chest and pulled the jumper over them as well as the skirt. Just as I was getting comfortable, Paula and Marie came walking around the corner. The fright I got! I nearly jumped out of my skin, Paula screaming about why I hadn't gone home, and Marie was shouting about the jumper being out of shape because it was over my legs. She hadn't noticed the cigarette burn, and I am sitting there thinking, *She's going on about the jumper; wait till she sees the skirt*. After all the shouting and screaming, they were both just relieved to find me. I still had the skirt business to contend with.

When I got in, I ran straight to the bathroom to get undressed and put the skirt at the bottom of the washing basket, naively thinking she wouldn't know it's there until it had been washed, and I could then blame the washing machine. We had a hand washing machine; it was years before we got a front loader, as they were called. Only people with money had them. I remember when phones first starting getting installed into houses. We got one when I was about fifteen. We used to sit waiting for it to ring and fall over each other trying to answer it.

Little did I know Marie already knew about the skirt, because she had already spoken to Tracey. She had told her about the skirt and how scared I was to go home. As mad as she was over it, she just wanted to get me home along with Paula. If I wasn't in at nine o'clock, as I got older, Paula would come looking for me and drag me home. Well, she said she did feel sorry for me, until she saw the jumper over my legs.

Another lesson for me I learned that day was to always take extra care of others' belongings, as well as appreciating the kindness Marie had shown me.

In every situation I have found myself in throughout my life, I have always taken lessons from it, whether it was teaching me something new or not to make the same mistake twice, as well as how deal with a situation. I have always believed learning is lifelong, and it is important to keep growing.

Chapter 12

Marie and I often look back on these memories and laugh about them. Only a couple of years ago, I told her what I used to do to earn extra money.

She worked two jobs; she always had money and the best clothes and make-up a girl could wish for. I would often parade around the room in her clothes, thinking, *I am going to be like her when I grow up.*

My mum didn't have many clothes when we were kids. Any money left over went on us. I would love to look in Marie's wardrobe and look at all the lovely dresses hanging up, picturing myself in them when I got older. That was the great thing about having older sisters: We all got tips off each other as what to buy and what to wear. We had our own personal dresser in each other.

She had so many clothes and shoes. Her room was quite untidy when she would leave for work. Quite often, she would say, 'If you clean my room, I will give you £2'. This was a lot at the time; this only happened now and again. Therefore, I had to come up with ways of earning money.

I wasn't getting it from my parents. I came up with the idea of untidying the room myself and then offering to tidy it for £1. I thought by offering it for £1 less, she was bound to agree. If she would have known at the time, she would have killed me.

In my eyes, this was the entrepreneur in me, trying to make money.

As well as working as a machinist, she had a second job in a bar. One night, she went out of the door to go to work, but she came running back in. She said, 'Ange, will you walk me to work? There are dogs outside, and I am scared of them'.

'I will if you pay me'.

She paid £2 for that good deed.

I was scared myself, but the thought of money far outweighed my fear of the dogs. On my way home, the money-making genius I thought I was came out. Just as the idea with the bedroom, I thought to myself, if them dogs are outside every time Marie has to go work, I could be paid.

From a very early age, I was always as wise as the hills. I had this money spent before I even earned it; no one could get anything past me. I would whistle them five minutes before she was due to go out, and lo and behold, she would come back in and ask me the same question.

She would have to pay me before I agreed to walk her. This went on for months. I had money to go to discos. I was very clever in the dogs I chose; just like all the kids played together, so did the dogs. They were like humans and even got the family surname when you spoke about them. There was Champ O'Donovan, that was a big red and beige sheep dog of my friend Debbie's, then there was Bingham Vaughan, a Kerry blue (he was called after Billy Bingham, the Everton manager at the time), there was also Sheeba Blackburn, a mongrel, so as you can imagine, these dogs were not the type that bite.

We never heard of pit bulls or Staffordshire bull terriers when were kids; these dogs would just walk around the estate all day long, not bothering anyone, except when I needed them.

When I told her a few years ago what I used to do, she said she knew what I was doing but wanted me to earn my own money. From an early age, she saw this as me earning what she was giving me. Here was me, thinking I was kidding her when she was the one doing it all along. Again, a lesson I learned was how to use my imagination to my advantage.

Chapter 13

Marie's work ethic, even at nineteen having two jobs to support herself as well as us, is what would give me the inspiration to grab the world with both hands and make the most of it from an early age, and this is what I strive to do each day.

My children are what have driven me on to ensure they had the opportunities I didn't, but my sister is the one who inspired me on how important it was to work hard. It wasn't just the lifestyle you desire when you have money, also the accomplishment in being successful. Being successful can also help you put something back and give to others less fortunate.

I look upon these experiences as learning for me to grow from as an individual and help shape me into becoming the person I am. As much as I thought I was being clever and wanting to earn money, even though it was wrong at the time, the biggest lesson was the independence she instilled in me to always work hard. She classed this as working, by walking her past the dogs and cleaning her bedroom, I knew from an early age you didn't get anything for nothing.

Chapter 14

My friends I grew up with on Radcliffe Walk were mostly like me, with big families.

Tracey had been my best friend from our first meeting in the friary infants when we were five, along with Tooty, Maxine, Debbie, and Marie, but Tracey and her family played a very big part in my growing up.

Whenever you went to her home, you were made to feel welcome. Joan and Tony showed me so much kindness throughout my childhood. My respect for them is still as strong today as it was all those years ago. I always imagined how my own family would be just like theirs.

I did go on to have three children, and just like the Birch household, mine has always been full of laughter and love for my boys to grow up in. The influences from my mum and dad along with my sisters and Tracey's family is how I was taught to raise a family.

As much as I wanted to always be successful from an early age, I always wanted to be the mum my own had been to us girls. My dad worked hard and always provided for us, but the bond between myself and my mum was so solid and the admiration I had for her, well, no one could compare.

Chapter 15

Often when we were growing up and my mum was short of money, we always knew my aunty Mary would be there to help us out.

We went to her house every Monday; all six of us would trot over to Queens Road. It was about a fifteen minute walk from where we lived. I looked forward to this every week; she and my uncle Albert had six children, one girl, Therese, and five boys. Even though their own house was full, they would never turn us away. Fig rolls along with a glass of orange juice was waiting for us, well as our cousins doing jigsaws, and we all joined in.

I adored this woman. Just like my mum, she always had a smile for us and again had shown us kindness when we needed it.

I still visited my aunty Mary right up until June 2007. She was the last of the Campbell family at seventy, and my mum (sixty-seven) was an age we were grateful for, compared to all our cousins who had lost one of their parents when they were all children. We count our blessings that our mum saw all her grandchildren born, and this is the reason I treasured her so much. We could so easily have been the ones growing up without her.

Chapter 16

Radcliffe Walk was a huge estate with big squares throughout, and the one we all congregated to was in the third block from where I lived. It was big enough to play rounders, football, hopscotch, and any other games we could think of.

At the bottom of the block was Gregson Street; it ran along the bottom of all the blocks. This was made up of maisonettes. They had one big communal garden and stairs that led down to Shaw Street Park. This is where we spent most of our childhood, as well as the hut that was in the park where we would go after school every night.

By the stairs that led to the park was a hill that the older kids had poured paint on and made a slide. Think of how kids used their imaginations to entertain themselves years ago. You don't see this anymore. We spent hours sliding down this hill and trying to run up it, to no avail. The laughs as we would come sliding back down you could hear throughout the estate.

The hut was run by Miss and Sir. Miss was little with red hair that looked like it had been shampooed and set every day; what an elegant woman, always pristine, and Sir was a stodgy, balding man who looked around sixty (he was probably nearer fifty).

Then there was Mr Leo; he was the cocky watchman, as he was known. He was an Italian man who guarded the park like his life depended on it. What fun we had in that park. This is where I learned to spin the ball when playing table tennis.

I played for hours, as well as in the summer, we would also get the stilts out and pretend we were in the circus.

The friendships that I made in this park carried on right throughout my childhood and are still there today.

This is where I first met Maxine, who I met when we were seven. I had been arguing with her brother Charles, and Maxine came to defend him. That first meeting started with two kids fighting, to going on to become friends for the last forty years. Maxine has also had her fair share of heartache, losing her husband Peter after two years of marriage and losing her daughter, baby Maxine, two years later, and just like my sister Kathy, she still found it within her to keep going. She went onto have three more children who are a credit to her.

Over the years, trips were arranged to different attractions, which we went to on a double decker. The most memorable was to Blackpool lights; packed lunches would more often than not be eaten by the time we got to the end of the street, leaving us all starving by the time we got there.

Looking back, I don't know how Miss and Sir coped with all the kids. They along with ordinary mums and dads would arrange these trips just to keep all the kids safe and occupied for the summer. This community may not have had a lot of money, but what it didn't have in that department, it more than made up for in terms of spirit, compassion, and empathy towards each other. What wonderful times were had in that park.

As we were getting older and the estate was changing, the slide disappeared. We would just find something else to occupy us. In the park was rocks that we thought were so big; it was like climbing Mount Everest, because we were that small.

Chapter 17

School for me started in the Friary infants, then leaving to attend SFX infant and junior school after only a few months, due to our move from the Four Squares.

That first day in school is imprinted in my mind forever. I only decided to go if Paula promised to pick me up. She agreed just to get me there.

I'll never forget sitting there, looking at the clock. I was able to tell the time from around three. Kathy sat me on her knee until I could recite it, so I knew it was closer to Paula coming for me, as I thought.

Off I went to the rail to get my coat, and as I glanced over my shoulder, it wasn't Paula picking me up but my dad. I ran right past him, crying, and through the back gate into Prince Edwin Street, screaming, 'Where's Paula?'

As he started running after me, there was a lady on her front path with her dog; she thought my dad was a stranger and set the dog on him. It was only his screams to get the dog off that made me turn around and run back up to him. Even though I wasn't happy to see him, I didn't want him to get bitten, and I also knew I was getting a belt for causing it.

The poor woman was mortified and thought she was getting reported. Just as well, my dad could understand her reasons for letting the dog out. I didn't just get a belt off him, but one off my mum too. The Friary would still be going when my two youngest were born. They also went to nursery there; my old teacher, Miss Loftus, was now the head teacher, who would still be dressed as perfectly as she was when I was there. Teachers along with the women of your family would influence you in more ways than you think.

After leaving the Friary, I was at SFX until I left for senior school. I was never really academically clever as a child. To achieve what I have in my career was more than I could ever imagine. I would never believe then I would be sitting here writing a book.

I was a very sporty child and excelled in gymnastics. I would do it at every opportunity and would sit for hours watching Olga Corbett and Nellie Kim, hoping one day to be like them. Because I was so tiny as a child, my frame was ideal.

I struggled throughout the juniors and seniors because of my lack of concentration levels and didn't learn much. The headmistress, Miss Cattrall, a big stern woman with bleach blonde hair, would often say in her posh accent, 'You, Angela Riley, will never amount to anything'. Looking back, I can understand why she said that.

I was outside her office door more than I was in the classroom, probably because I couldn't understand the work. I would often kick up a fuss, so no one knew the real reason behind me not wanting to learn.

In those days, there were no mentors or classroom assistants to help kids like me; we were just seen as class clowns. I often wonder was I dyslexic and that was the reason for avoiding learning at all costs?

As she was telling me I would amount to nothing, I still remember standing there saying in my mind, *I may never be a teacher, but whatever I choose to do, I will succeed at it.* What I lacked academically I more than made up for with passion and have always put my heart and soul into everything I have ever done. This is what would always bring me success.

I thought about this teacher when I decided to write this book and would have loved to let her know I did listen to what she tried to teach me, did go on to learn academically, although my biggest success has always been my children. I believe they are our biggest accomplishments in life. My children have all gone on to serve children less fortunate than themselves. For me, this is my biggest accolade.

From SFX, I went on to St Michael's senior school in Mill Road, a mixed school which was quite strange and hard to adapt to, as I had only ever known all-girls schools. Just like the junior school, I found it hard academically and again would go on to shine in sport. I finally got badges for gymnastics, which were sewn onto a black leotard.

That feeling of accomplishment was when I first realised how good it felt to achieve the ultimate and have something to show for it. This is when that fire in my belly got stronger for wanting more. I was getting older and realising how good it felt to stand out. Netball was something else I was very good at. I played centre, and because I was little and skinny, I was all over the field. Just like when I was a child, tipping the board over when I got beaten, I wouldn't take it well when we got beaten as a team.

I always had that yearning to be good at something, whether it was playing in goal in Radcliffe Walk (I got nicknamed Bruce Grobbelaar; as thin as I was, I had big knees), to gymnastics and netball in senior school. When you're a child growing up, you never really take education serious. That is why I ensured my own children had a good education.

Not learning could have had a detrimental effect on my future. This is also the reason I have chosen to become a parent and youth impact coach.

I believe if children have support from a parent or guardian, they can go on to be and do anything they want.

It is my belief they can excel at anything they put their mind to; today's children are tomorrows future leaders, prime ministers, doctors, and nurses. If we are to educate children, it is important for parents to also be educated, to help nurture the talent that runs through every child. It is our job as adults to find this and help it grow. Children are like plants; if you water them regularly, this helps the roots to grow, and that is exactly what we must do with children. We must push them to be the best version of themselves, always growing and reaching for more.

Chapter 18

When I left school, I drifted from one job to another. I started off on a government scheme that paid twenty-five pounds per week, simply because I had left school with very few qualifications, so getting a decent job was out of the question.

I did various roles from cleaning to silver service waitress, as well as working in factories and shops, also looking after the elderly. Although at the time of doing these jobs I enjoyed them, I also knew I wanted more fulfilment in my job and these roles were not fulfilling my need inside, nor did they ever tax my brain.

On leaving the scheme after only six months, I went to work in a printers on the Dock Road; that more than doubled my wages. I remember being so excited because I would still have forty-three pounds per week left after paying keep. I could buy all sorts with that, mainly make-up and clothes.

The first place I went was to a hairdressers in London Road called Snips and got my brown hair dyed blonde. I used to watch *Charlie's Angels* and loved Farrah Fawcett's hair. I got my hair done exactly like hers. Years later, Barry joked when I came out of the hairdresser's how I looked like Farrah Fawcett. He forgot I told him the story years before and thought he was complimenting me.

My next stop was of course to Next. I had waited years to go into this shop; my goodness, it felt good to finally buy something from there. I felt like a million dollars buying clothes from that store. I remember standing outside the shop with the biggest smile on my face, saying to myself, *I did it*. It was at that moment I always knew I would do what I set my heart on.

In all of the jobs I went in and out of, I never once got that sense of belonging until years later. I lasted eighteen months working in the printers and again was on the move. This time I was working with the elderly; although it was rewarding, my job was to shop for them and just sit with them, providing company. I still felt I had more to give.

Chapter 19

I met Barry at nineteen, although i had known him since i was fourteen, and was still drifting from job to job until I had my first child at twenty-two.

Bringing Christopher home to our one-bedroom flat is still so clear in my memory.

I looked at him and thought back to the promises I made to myself when I was a child, just like my own parents had started off with Kathy in a one-room flat.

I made a decision that day that my Christopher was never going without. My parents had provided what they could for us, but still we went without so much, and I could not allow the same for mine.

When we moved into the flat we were living in, I had to borrow the money from my boss at the time to pay for furniture and then work for six weeks with no pay. We were given a fridge as well as a second-hand suite, but this flat was ours, and we made it home until Christopher was born. Yes, of course, I wanted Christopher to have everything I hadn't, but most importantly, I wanted to be the mum mine had been to me and guide and protect him as he grew, as well as instilling confidence in him to believe anything was possible. Ensuring he always had my support was my first priority.

I fully understood now that feeling inside to protect. My mum had displayed this when we were all kids. It was on show for all to see. The wind couldn't blow on him, I was that protective, so imagine the fear that ran through me when Christopher was nine days old and suffering from colic. I gave him what I thought was gripe water; it turned out to be witch hazel. I will never forget the fright I got when the midwife told me she would have to phone Guy's Hospital in London for advice on what to do. She did make light of the situation in the end. She could see how afraid I was. She informed me he'd have a hangover the next morning.

I wanted the same relationship with my children my own mum had with us. The love, compassion, and empathy I felt from her set me up and gave me the confidence to believe in my own abilities and achieve.

So life settled down as before Christopher was born. I had a couple of years off to look after him whilst Barry worked. I always knew I wasn't cut out to just be a housewife, and if Christopher wasn't to go without, we would need two wages coming in. Even though I wasn't feeling fulfilled in all the jobs I had done, I learned life skills in all of them. The most important skill for me was people skills, that I used to help guide people when needed. All of these skills would serve me well in later years when working in a finance company.

I started work when Christopher was around two in a shop called Home and Bargain. Barry was also working there as the security guard. I only worked part time, so as I was still there for him when he needed me, my mum looked after Christopher until he started nursery, when he was three.

Again, having a child was not going to stop me paving my own path as well as learning new skills. I carried on with this job until I became pregnant with Leighton, my second child. I had to pack up work early due to complications, so I found myself with no income of my own, meaning we would have to live on one wage. Again, I thought back to being a child and the promises I made about my own children. These memories are what have always spurred me on to keep going, and that is why I will never regret one single moment of my childhood, as the same struggles that we all faced gave me the courage and determination to always reach for more.

Chapter 20

Car boot sales had just started in Liverpool, and people were making good money from selling their old goods. I thought, why not do the same. I gathered all Christopher's old clothes as well as old furniture and curtains that were no longer being used. Barry and I set off at four in the morning; we had been told to get there early to get a good spot.

That first Sunday, we made over two hundred pounds. Twenty-two years ago, that was a lot of money, so that's when it hit me. I was still able to earn, plus it was more than I had earned in my part-time job, so I decided I would gather all the unwanted items my family had and would go to the car boot each Sunday.

The site was on waste ground on the Dock Road. As the weeks went on, I could see what other stall holders were doing. They would walk around and buy off stalls and then put the items in their own stall the following week. We were by now running out of items, so decided to do the same. The majority of items were really dirty or broken. We would take them home, clean them, fix them, and sell them on at a profit.

Then we found out about summer fayres, jumble sales, and Christmas fair; we would spend hours in queues waiting for the doors to open and get the best bargains. The negotiating skills we both learned from these sales were second to none. I would get items for as little as five pence and sell them on with a huge profit.

The longer we were at the boot sale, we got to know more and more people. In addition to there being a lot of traders going around, there was also antique dealers who would try and kid you if you didn't know how much something was worth. You could actually lose a lot of money, but my husband had an eye for antiques and was very good at knowing one antique from another, so we learnt very quickly how to barter. We didn't just save money on what we bought, but we also made more than the average on what we sold.

Everything we bought was scrubbed with jiff until it looked brand new; this is why we had repeat customers. They also knew they could return it and get their money back if they wasn't happy.

This income was now becoming a regular wage. I was earning on average of three hundred pounds a week. This was not just providing the necessities, but also luxuries and holidays, which considering I was working only a Sunday and a few hours Friday and Saturday going to jumble sales, it was a whole lot more than I had been getting working part time. We were now taking this seriously and were thinking with business minds. Barry and his brother opened a second stall selling confectionary; to think this was all started through selling unused items. I also had a trader who came to my stall every Sunday and bought the bulk of goods to sell on in his shop. I would more than double the profit alone from the sale to him.

I knew by cleaning all the items, my customer base would quadruple, even if I did spend Saturday nights scrubbing it all.

We continued with the car boot sales for a couple more years and made a very good living from it. We also started working on Wednesdays. My sister Tricia and my mum would be looking after Christopher and Leighton; this gave us a lifestyle that normally only came with working full time. The saying where there is muck there is money certainly worked for us. It also worked perfectly, because it meant I was there most of the time with my kids.

Finally, after three years and with my third son Joseph coming along, we got the news that would shatter us: The car boot sale was to close and become a truck stop. This was devastating, as not only was it a business, it also fitted in with family life.

We just couldn't believe it was closing, but at the same time, we had a good run from it and decided there and then no matter what, we had been used to earning this money and that wouldn't stop. We would just have to come up with something else. I was now looking for my next project but wasn't sure what; as before, my problem was always my lack of education, so it was time to get my thinking cap on.

Chapter 21

After giving birth to Joseph, I decided to pick up driving lessons again, as I had given them up when I found out I was pregnant with Leighton. Now I had to seriously think of the future. It was time to start them again. The way I looked at it, what I lacked academically, by passing my test and getting a car, new doors would certainly open for me.

After passing my test and using the money we had saved from the car boot sales, I had enough money to buy my first car. Now I was back in business. My goodness, my own car! Who would have thought it? I had never even owned a bike, and here I was with my own car. No one would have believed that.

I felt like I had wings; now, anything was possible. The independence and confidence that came with passing my test was fantastic.

Not long after my sister-in-law had started working for a loan company as an agent, she kept on at me about doing the same. This was a doorstep loan company that offered credit to customers with payment on a weekly basis.

Like the car boot sale, it fitted in with family life. I kept saying no, I wasn't interested, then after talking to Barry's cousin, who also worked for the same company, I decided I would give it a go. It was only for a couple of hours per day on Friday and Monday, and you could earn in excess of three hundred pounds per week. Well, that was serious money. This is what I had been earning in the car boot sales.

I knew I wouldn't get this kind of income straight away; you had to work at it and build up your customer base to earn top commission. The more customers you had to sell to, the more commission you could earn.

Christopher was now five, Leighton was just under two, and Joseph was three months old. My mum would look after the boys until Barry finished work at four thirty. I started off earning fifty pounds per week on what was called a scratch book; this was made up of about fifty customers.

It was nowhere near what I had been told you could earn, but I knew if I worked at it, it wouldn't be long before I was making more. It took a couple of years to start earning the three hundred pounds. I knew this was the job for me. I built up the agency by word of mouth and cold calling to sign up new customers. As hard as it was to knock on doors and sometimes get abuse, I knew if I was to earn the money I had been earning previously, I had to take every opportunity offered. I loved meeting new people. The way I looked at it, I was providing a service. I wasn't just an agent to my customers, I saw them as friends and would often attend christenings, weddings, and even funerals. I would be going to their houses every week, so I got to know them quite well. I was at this company for just under three years.

I went on holiday for three weeks and on my return, another agent had covered it whilst I was on holiday, resulting in it going down. After me building this agency up over three years for it to go right down was heart-breaking for me. I had put my heart and soul into it. I felt I had no option but to leave.

I have always set goals for myself; the reason for working so hard on the agency was the goal I had set to take my boys to Disneyland in Florida. I was really upset leaving the job I had loved, but I was so angry that resigning seemed like the only choice. I was so annoyed that all the hard work I put into it had gone undone.

Whilst I had been working as an agent, a manager's job became available, and due to how I had done on the agency, I thought that would put me in good stead. I decided to apply for it. The manager's role was to discuss payment options with customers who had fallen into difficulty with repayments, as well as support the agents where needed.

I found this side of the role quite easy because of how I spoke to my own customers, and more often than not, I would do my own arrears work on the agency, so here I was, thinking I stood as good a chance as anyone if not better. Every week I went in for what was called an interview with your manager. I was always informed of how well I was doing, so I naturally thought this would be a good sign, plus the role of an agent was no longer giving me that inner feeling of fulfilment. I was finding myself out growing it.

I believed it was now time to move to the next level. My children were also older, and Joseph was now in nursery, so a manager's job could still fit in with my family life.

When I went into the area manager's office, the response I got was so different to what I had expected. His reply to my enquiry knocked me for six: 'Go on a communication skills course, and then I may consider you for an interview'. Anyone who knows me would tell you I could have a degree in communicating, I talk that much.

That was probably the best recommendation I ever had throughout my career. As I stood in his office, I remember thinking, *I won't just be a manager, I will one day sit in your chair.*

I now made it my business to educate myself and make him eat his words. It was only later on after becoming a manager I realised he wasn't having a go. There is a way in which you should communicate in business, and I had to learn this before I could move forward, but that was to be the finest piece of advice I was ever given.

Chapter 22

That determination to become a manager was now my next biggest focus after my children, and after leaving with no other job lined up, I was still determined I would one day get what I promised myself in his office.

I left in October 1996 and didn't work until after Christmas.

I went on to work as a cleaner in an office in Rodney Street, not just cleaning offices, but also toilets. The thing that kept me going was my vision of becoming a manager. I also knew this was just a means to an end and would have done anything to pay my way and put food on the table for my children, as well as my rent. The rent at the time was twenty-nine pounds fifty pence. The house was a two up, two down in a terraced street with only four houses in; the neighbours were the salt of the earth, who would look after the house when we went on holiday, always looking out for each other.

Our house was the only rented one in the street. Imagine what they must have been like when it became vacant through the death of the old man. These neighbours still live in that street today. They raised all their children there.

I remember that first day getting the key to go and look at the house along with Barry, my sister Michelle, and her husband Joseph.

Michelle has always had an eye for interior design, and the two of us were so excited at what I could do to it. My goodness, the plans I had for my very first home. The flat was comfortable, but this was a house with a dining room and a yard for Christopher to play in. Things I only dreamt of as a child, I could now buy for him. I would have a place to put them all, even a swing and a slide. I had to go to the park if I wanted to go on a swing when I was a child.

All of these thoughts running through my mind, my sister in the background designing each room, again this was the empathy that we felt towards each other from little girls, always getting excited if one of us got something new. I was that delighted at the thought of us getting this house, I didn't want to give the key back in case they changed their mind.

We moved in January 1990, and this was to be the best decision we made. When you walked into the street, you could feel the sense of belonging, along with the peace and quiet. Even though we were the only ones renting, we felt part of our own lovely little community. We were never made to feel any less acceptable than the neighbours. Both Leighton and Joseph were born in the house.

I carried on working in Rodney Street for a couple of months, disliking every minute, but I knew I had to keep going whilst looking for something else.

One day, reading the *Liverpool Echo,* an advertisement jumped out at me: collecting agent required for doorstep lending company. I was all excited ringing the number. Although it said no experience required, I had nearly three years and thought this would help me secure an interview. From there, I would do my utmost to get the job.

I already knew I enjoyed this type of job as being able to earn a large income, and more importantly, even though I was going backwards becoming an agent, I have always believed sometimes we have to take a step back to get us to where we want to be, and that was to be a manager.

Just like my previous job, this provided cash loans as well as high street vouchers. I could relate to the customers. Just like mine, most families in Liverpool were brought up with vouchers and cheques paying for clothes and some household essentials. You could pay weekly. Families with small children relied on this service.

I had never actually heard of this company until I started working there, so when I was going for the interview, I did have second thoughts about going, but I decided to just go and check it out.

When I walked into that office in Aintree and heard lots of laughter, I felt comfortable straight away. The previous company was a big organisation. This had more of a family feel about it. There was no difference from the branch manager. He was a lovely guy, always smiling, with a really strong Scottish accent (sometimes I was unable to understand him). He had an open door policy; that taught me to do the same years later. He taught me that from the clerical staff to the agents, everyone was important to the success of the branch.

I got the job and as before took on an agency with around fifty customers that were spread all over Liverpool. The difference was, these were longstanding customers who had a relationship with the company for years.

I was taking over from a lady who was retiring after thirty-two years' service, so the customers were of course weary. They had arranged set times with the previous agent; I certainly had big shoes to fill.

The first three weeks was spent with the manager, who introduced me to the customers. The first couple of weeks didn't go very well, simply because these customers looked on the previous agent as family. They probably felt like they were betraying her, but I didn't let that put me off. I thought, *I won't even try to take her place, I will be myself and build a relationship with each and every one of them, and just as I had thought all those years ago, when I went to the solicitors, I'm here now, so I might as well try.*

I was only earning seventy pounds per week when I first started; you may wonder why I left my previous job where I was earning more, but I left on principle, so even though it wasn't much more than the cleaning job, it was a job I enjoyed, and I also knew how good I was at it, as well as what the earning potential was. That is what got me excited at the thought of a new beginning.

The hours were Monday to Friday with Wednesday off. Because this was a well-established agency, the hours I would be working were school hours. They were perfect for me.

I was able to take my sons to school as well as pick them up. I have never once missed a parents evening nor a Christmas panto or Mother's Day assembly. It has always been so important for me to encourage my children in everything they did.

I always ensured I was available to support them at all times. I felt that creating this type of environment for my boys to grow up in would help them excel on their chosen path.

As time went on and the customers started to accept and trust me for who I was, I became a counsellor, a teacher, a nurse, and most importantly a friend, bearing in mind some of these people had been customers as long as the previous agent had been with the company. For them to welcome me into their homes meant the world to me. Sometimes, I was the only person some of these customers saw, so I would give them time and listen to them when they needed to talk. This would sometimes make me late to my next customer. They would then ring me to make sure I was okay, and if they couldn't get me, they would ring Barry, worrying about me.

Chapter 23

Certain customers still stick in my mind today; there was a family I went to every Tuesday, three generations who were so lovely, and after going there as usual one Tuesday, sitting and talking for twenty minutes, to the following Thursday, getting a phone call telling me the nan had been killed in a house fire the night before.

I was devastated over this loss, as I got to know this lady over the months. She would make me laugh with her tales and stories. Although they were customers, they were inviting you into their home. The least I could do was show them respect and have empathy towards them.

I was providing a service for them, and I appreciated that, but they provided me with more than just a good income. The death of that lovely lady affected me more than I thought it would.

They weren't the only friends I made in the job. I also went to see a lady in the Albert Dock who no longer needed the loans but got them out of habit. I would sit and have a few coffees with her every Tuesday before my next call was due. When she went on holiday and didn't pay for a couple of weeks, you would guarantee I would have two bad weeks.

This being commission based, I had to collect well to earn good commission; a bad week meant low commission.

There was also the family in Croxteth, where every Thursday I could smell the dinner as I walked up the path. It was like a bisto advertisement. Just the smell made me hungry.

They would have a plate of Cumberland sausage and mash with gravy waiting for me. Then there was another very special lady who thought that much of me, she rang one morning near Christmas to tell me not to call. She had been informed I was going to be mugged; because I collected a lot of money, I was always going to be a target. She put herself on the line to warn me, and I was forever in debt to her for this. This could have affected me in a big way. These customers became like family to me, so much so, I would often buy their little ones Easter eggs and other gifts, and my sons would get the same back.

Chapter 24

This agency became a business to me. I built it over the years. At the time of starting, I was thinking of it just being for a while, until I could look at going back into education. I had always dreamt of becoming a journalist. My dad had nicknamed me Kate Aidy, because I always had a story to tell, along with Kathy calling me Hans Christian Anderson. It was only natural that I should go down the path of writing a book. That dream was to stay just a dream. As the weeks and months turned into years, I was earning far too much commission to give it up, and that is what I would have had to do if I followed my dream.

I just put it on hold until such time as now, when I am able to follow my heart and do the job I believe I was born to do. That is another reason for writing this book: to show others that with self-belief along with determination and support, you can achieve anything you set your heart on.

As well as cash loans and high street vouchers, we also sold goods from a catalogue. I would be given a target to reach. The goods that were sold would generate a commission base along with the normal collecting commission, although as competitive as I am, I would only ever sell what the customer wanted and needed. More often than not, I would try to talk them out of it. They were more than just customers. Just as my own mum had been grateful all those years before, my customers were also grateful to be able to have the things they could only have dreamt of otherwise.

Time went on, and I started to get itchy feet again. I was becoming bored in the role. I constantly like to be challenged. Although the money was very good and hours were perfect, it just wasn't taxing my brain. I needed a fresh challenge.

I went into the manager's office and asked him about going into management. He looked at me with amazement and asked why I would go into management when I was earning so much as an agent. I advised him, as I have advised others since, money has never been my motivation in life. Inner peace and fulfilment in my job is what has always been important to me.

He was quick to tell me how well I was doing and I should continue as an agent. I stood there thinking to myself, *You would say that because I was bringing the results in, so why would you want to change that?* I pointed out to him, 'Wouldn't you gain more if I was teaching others the tricks of the trade? As a manager, my responsibility would be to ensure all agents were trained to the highest level'.

His reply was, 'At the moment, we have no vacancies, but I will keep this conversation in mind, and if anything comes up, I'll let you know'.

He must have slept on it; the next day, he called me in and said he had a proposal for me.

He said, 'I've been thinking about yesterday's conversation; how would you feel about becoming a buddy agent?'

My first thought was, that's not the same as a manager's job, so why would I be interested? I thought I'd give him the benefit of the doubt and hear him out; he offered me £20 a day for every agent I trained.

I worked four days per week, so every agent who came through the door, this was an extra £80 per week. It was very good money. By training individuals, it would make my day a lot longer, so I had to decide if it was worth it. I knew why he had come up with this idea: in case I left. I informed him the day before I was no longer enjoying the role.

I decided to sleep on it and let him know the next day. After talking it through with Barry, I decided to take the offer. At the end of the day, I was definitely a people person, and to train others, this was a skill most definitely needed.

The rewards and the inner feeling of fulfilment were worth the long days; also, the extra money came in handy.

I was constantly training. As I finished with one, there would be another one waiting. This just made my hunger for management even stronger. It was great to watch someone grow from that first nervous day to becoming a fully fledged agent earning top commission and loving what they were doing. As a manager, this is what my role would consist of, as well as supporting them with non-payment accounts. That burning inside kept growing stronger.

When I look back, I was probably earning more than a newly qualified journalist and was actually only working fifteen hours per week. I was now enjoying the training so much, if there was a week I wasn't training, the job would feel monotonous. I would just be going through the motions. Yes, the money was fantastic, yet I still had to fill that void feeling inside I had felt for a long time. After training, I knew this was my niche.

After training agents for six months, my area manager suddenly left and in came a new one. She decided to pull the plug on the daily payment and advised I would only get £20 per week for training. Although it wasn't about money, I wasn't going to carry on doing the same job for £60 per week less.

Chapter 25

I decided I really needed a change now the training had finished. Although it could have had disastrous effects on not just myself but also my family, I knew it had to be done.

I have always known when it is time to walk away from a job. I also have so much belief in my own abilities and the decisions I make. This was no different; my drive and enthusiasm, as well as my passion for success, have always taken me forward.

There was also another reason for wanting management: I had been looking at houses. Our current home was getting too small. The boys were older, and with all the toys they had accumulated over the years, it was becoming smaller. With only two bedrooms, the three of them were in one room. It was a complete squash, so was only a matter of time before we had to move.

I had already been in touch with the housing trust to discuss building an extension or selling the property to us, and they had said yes, we could build an extension; however, the rent would go from £29.50 per week to £45.00, and no there wasn't an option of buying.

I wasn't prepared to lay out cost for something that would eventually cost me more money with the extra rent. I now knew I had to look elsewhere.

Before looking for a property, we spoke to the bank manager about a mortgage. He advised us it would be much more difficult to get one if I was self-employed. My husband's salary alone wasn't enough to get the houses we were thinking of. Even though I had accounts and my commission was very good, it would still be a problem. I was classed as high risk.

One night driving home from my mum's, I decided to go into the sales office of a new build on Everton Road. 'Just to look', I told Barry. 'Yes, okay?'

Barry's reply was, 'We can't afford them'.

Me, as usual, said, 'We'll just look'.

We went into the office, and the sales rep advised there was only the show house left, the majority of goods, along with the front and back garden all designed was in with the price. This meant it was more expensive than the rest. With that, Barry walked out.

I pulled him back and asked, 'What is the harm in looking? We can get a few ideas'.

He was still trying to change my mind as I was opening the front door to the house, that stubbornness once more showing itself as it has done right throughout my life to follow my heart. I carried on walking in, still hearing Barry's voice in my head trying to talk me out of it.

The feeling I got when I walked into that hallway was what would drive me towards my goal of management.

I was even more determined. Now I wanted this house so much. I stood in each room, picturing us in there, and I could hear my boys' laughter throughout. I dared to dream that this could be possible if only I could be employed. Everything about this house made my desire even stronger to have it.

When I walked into the garden, I pictured my boys playing and running around. That vision in my mind's eye was so strong, I made a decision that would have Barry screaming. Not even the bank manager's voice ringing in my ears put me off.

I decided there and then to put down a deposit of £100, which was non-refundable. Barry told me we couldn't afford to lose any money.

I told him, 'Don't worry, we won't'. Again that belief in myself as strong as ever, also the fear of losing the money is what kept me dreaming. It was two minutes from my mum's house and five from Barry's. It just got better. If I asked Barry today was it a good idea going into that house, he would probably say no, because that became my focus from then on to get it.

Even a little thing as being self-employed was not going to get in my way. My mission started with speaking to the sales rep at Wimpey on who would be the best person for a mortgage.

He recommended a guy in Long Lane Fazakerley. Even if he told us it was impossible, I still probably wouldn't have accepted it. I was now desperate to have this house. None of the trials and tribulations we went through, as well as the hurdles put in front of us at the time, put me off.

I wanted my boys to be left with something after I was gone, from all the hard work Barry and I had done. A house to share between them was only the beginning.

This guy, his name is engraved in my memory, it was Phil Jones, and just like the bank manager before, he told us it would be difficult but not impossible. That glimmer of hope kept me going. If we went through one broker, we went through ten, and Barry, trying to protect me, suggested, 'Why don't we just leave it and go for something more affordable?'

The answer I often gave was, 'I am not giving up, I know it's meant for us'.

After what seemed like months, we were finally accepted by a company called Platform 7, although not your average broker, and the repayments were more.

Oh my goodness, we had finally done it. Now we just had to get the deposit together, which was about five thousand pounds. The majority we had saved up, but to cover the legal fees, I sold all my jewellery to ensure nothing was going to stop us. Because we were high risk, this was another reason we had to go with this lender. If our circumstances were to change, then we could look at the High Street when it was time to swop it over, reducing the monthly payments by more than half.

We were finally going to own our own home. My mum and dad would be so proud, proving that even leaving school with the basic of education doesn't stop you from achieving and making the most of life.

I will never forget 16 August 1999, the day we got the keys. We were now on the property ladder. What an achievement; my optimism had paid off. How proud was I. We carried on with our dream when it seemed like everything was against us. It was like winning the lottery ten times over. I still remember Barry's words: 'I am so glad you didn't listen to me, Ange'. I didn't tell him at the time I was more worried than I was letting on.

Due to me working late, Barry along with Michelle and Joseph moved everything in.

I still recall sitting outside my house that day, just thinking back to my childhood. Who would have thought when I was wearing hand-me-downs and not even owning a doll, to now getting ready to move into my own home?

Barry's childhood wasn't as hard as mine. It didn't seem as exciting for him, but he was delighted for us as a family. I walked in after working all day. I couldn't believe what Michelle had done. She had everything in its place, even the food in the cupboards and beds all made up. It looked like we had always lived there, with empty boxes in the garden, ready for the bin men. I cried with excitement and joy that we had finally done it.

I had prayed so hard for this house, and now all I had to do was thank God for my blessings. I believe gratitude is so important and was always grateful for anything I got, even the top all those years ago from Joan. When I sat at the table with a Malibu to celebrate watching the kids playing in the garden, I thought of how we had done it all for them. All the love, warmth, and laughter was now transferred from our old home to the new one.

Waking up with the sun shining into my bedroom was the most amazing sight to see; all that had been instilled in me as a little girl had shown itself when I needed it most. My love and admiration for my parents just grew after that day.

As hard as our childhood had been, I had so much to thank them for; we were far more richer for the morals and values they had instilled in each and every one of us. My determination is what got us that house and my will to win. Not giving up when the going got tough was the big factor in buying our first home and the support of my lovely sister in making sure it went without a hitch. She knew it would be difficult for me. She decided she would make sure by hook or by crook we would move in on that day. Once again that bond showed itself when needed.

A few weeks after the new manager's arrival, I decided to go and speak to her about management. After our conversation, she said she would have a think about the way forward, where we were both happy, and would get back to me. I was happy with that, as she was taking me seriously. She had listened to what I had said. I couldn't have asked for more. She had already looked at where I had taken my own agency from as well as the training of the new recruits. I felt I had to give her a chance to see what she came up with. I knew it was difficult, because there wasn't actually any vacancies.

The manager called me into the office the following day. As before, she came up with another proposal to split my agency into two. I would train the two new agents and rather than my role just being management, it would also consist of recruiting customers and agents as well as training them. Although she had initially taken away the training fee I had been getting, the offer she put on the table was better than I could have imagined.

I was to be a training manager, but I was getting a contract, and that meant employment, and my salary would be going straight into my account, which is exactly what we wanted and needed if we were to change our mortgage. There was one problem: It was less than I was earning as an agent, although the role did come with a car, which meant I could sell mine and release some cash, as well as saving on petrol, tax, and insurance, so I had to speculate to accumulate. I asked her could I speak to my husband, as I didn't know whether the drop in salary would be a problem, especially with it not long after moving into the new house.

On speaking to Barry about my options, his answer, as always, was, 'Do what you need to do'. His support has always been there on every decision I made. Even if he didn't agree with it at the time, he said, 'If we have to substitute things to help us progress, then we will plan accordingly, and I will also work extra hours to make up for what you lose'.

As much as I am determined and driven to succeed, his faith in me never wavered; having him behind me is what has always pushed me on. He said, 'The reason for this is how I get things done and the belief I have that you can achieve anything'. He said I never fail to amaze him. When I set my sights on something, I will not be defeated.

The fear of failure is always vivid in my mind; although my vision and optimism always paid off, I find myself always striving for more. My reasons behind my continued growth are my boys and the influence it will have on their decisions and their futures.

Chapter 26

The decision was made, and I was giving my beloved agency up. I found it much harder than I thought; losing contact with my customers was going to be a lot more difficult than I had suspected.

I had to think of the effect it would have on them. I had one week to let them all know what was happening. These customers had built the trust up in me; now I was leaving them. I felt like I was letting them down.

No more Tuesdays in the Dock or sausage and mash on a Thursday, as well as the lovely family in West Derby. Besides these three families, there were others that had a big effect on me. One woman in particular had a huge impact on my life.

She had moved into my area because of domestic violence. God, I wondered how anyone could even shout at this woman, never mind hit her. She was so frail and quiet. I felt physically sick when she told me what she had been through.

This lady had hardly any furniture but always greeted me with a smile. I felt I had been her confidant; she found someone to offload to.

One week I got there, she told me her daughter's pram had broken, and she had no money to replace it. Even though I needed my own pram for Joseph, I knew I had to give it to her. As I went over to the boot and took it out, she was looking at me, wondering what I was doing. When I handed that pram to her, she was in such shock she couldn't speak. Her little boy was standing next to her holding onto her leg, not much younger than Christopher.

This child had witnessed so much and had even suffered deafness through shock. I was so grateful my own children had never witnessed this.

I thought back to when I was a child and thought that was bad enough, so God only knows what this child had seen.

Although she never had much, she never missed a payment and could so easily have kept the payment to buy a pram, but she had decided otherwise, so that was why I gave her mine. I had done what Joan had done all those years before and gave a little bit of what I had, and that is the greatest feeling in the world –to share what you have with others.

When I got home and told Barry about the pram, his first reaction was to get annoyed, but then as I explained these same people have helped us to buy a house, never missing their accounts, meaning I always earned good commission.

If I could give a little bit back, I should; he calmed down and then wanted to know what else we could do for her. That night, we looked at what clothes Christopher had that we could share with this lady's little boy. Some of them he still wore. I felt he could get by without them, and anyway I didn't have many when I was his age. It didn't do me any harm. That's what happened on a regular basis. I always felt the need to give back, feeling grateful for what I had. Although it was my job and I worked hard, my customers were so loyal and very rarely missed their payments, so it was important to give something back.

Chapter 27

I started my new position, supposedly as a training manager, still feeling unsatisfied inside; I felt I was only a glorified agent with a car.

I continued this for a while, not getting any real satisfaction from the role; however, I also knew I couldn't just walk away this time. If I was to get a mortgage with my own bank, I would just have to see it out until something better came up. If ever there was a time I questioned my decisions, this was one of them.

I absolutely detested every day I had to spend in this job. I felt like I had been hoodwinked into giving my agency up by being promised the role I was getting would lead to management. Looking back later on, I knew they had given me this role to stop me leaving, knowing full well it would not lead to anything more. I also knew I couldn't let this get to me and still kept that optimism of one day being a real manager, not forgetting that conversation a few years before in my old area manager's office is what stopped me walking out on many occasions.

After a few months in this role, a manager's position became available in the sister company. I was invited for an interview and came away feeling elated because the interview had gone so well. The man who interviewed me all but said that I had the job.

I slept well that night, convinced I had done enough to secure the position; imagine my shock when I got a phone call the next day, informing me I had been unsuccessful. That phone call nearly crushed me. I remember standing in my living room, crying and saying to Barry, 'I will never get my break'.

I had worked so hard to impress people; what more could I do? I just didn't know where to turn. As always, Barry was there with his words of comfort: 'Ange, you will get what you want in the end, just keep believing'.

I had a day of feeling sorry for myself, and then it was time to dust myself down and move on.

Chapter 28

True enough, as Barry had said, only months later, I finally got my break. All my hard work and willpower was finally paying off. I got a manager's job with another home credit company. My title was assistant branch manager. I couldn't believe I had finally done it. My dream of becoming a manager had happened. Who would have thought this little girl who left school learning very little would amount to this? My vision was still within my sights, and now would work hard to achieve this.

I have always felt the need to dream big. As someone once told me, 'If your dreams don't scare you, they aren't big enough'. I always set my sights high.

I remember the first time I saw a letter being sent out to a customer offering them credit with my name on it – how excited I was at that. This may seem trivial to some people. For me, it was the proof I had been successful in my quest for management.

I would often be driving to the office after dropping my boys off at school, thanking God for my blessings and still feeling so grateful for what I had.

I was responsible for managing and supporting a team of ten agents; like the customers, these agents were everything to me. I was now receiving a very good salary and drove a company car.

I gave it my all to support every agent when I could. They relied on me to provide guidance when needed, ensuring they were earning the highest commission possible. Also, I had promised the regional manager at my interview I would be the best manager he would ever recruit.

I was the first woman manager he appointed to his team. I had a point to prove that I was as good as any man, if not better.

His actual words at the time were, 'Why should I give you the job? This is normally a man's job'.

My reply was, 'Well, it obviously hasn't worked with men or you wouldn't be interviewing me. I believe it is about time you took a chance on a woman, and that woman should be me'.

I believe my cheekiness and straight talking is what got me my job. I never let him down. I went on to become a top-performing manager, winning not just customer promotions but also performance competitions. I was always up there with the rest of them.

I had done the role of the agent so could relate to each of them and all the issues they had. I would quite quickly resolve any problems they had. By being this type of manager, I always got the best out of them by gaining their respect (even though the majority were older than me).

All of my agents were important to me. I had three who would go on to become more than just agents; two friends who had worked for the company for around thirty years; and just as I had when I was an agent, they treated it as a business.

I could always rely on them to go over and beyond for me. They went on to become friends of mine, along with another agent I had taken on and trained (her husband was my husband's foreman).

I never in my wildest dreams thought she would not only be one of the best agents I trained but also play a major part in a life-changing decision.

I was at this company from October 2000 until November 2003 and can honestly say I loved every day I worked there. Even though I was now working in excess of fifty hours per week, it still didn't stop me enjoying it. As tired as I sometimes got, I would get a kick out of the problem solving that came with the role and seeing the end result. I also knew if I was to be the best I could be, then this was the sacrifice I had to make. As much as I worked that long, I never once compromised my time with my family. I made sure I was always available and fitted the job around my family life. That is why it worked well for me.

Chapter 29

Wednesday, 18 December 2002, was the start of what I can only describe as the worst year possible; this was the day Chris, my father-in-law, was diagnosed with cancer, which was devastating for the whole family.

Barry didn't know how to cope with this news. The man he had looked up to all his life and helped shape him into the person he is today was not going to get better. Chris played such a big part in his life, that he was Barry's best man when we got married.

I remember the day he told me who would be standing next to him on our wedding day. I was shocked; I had never heard of anyone having their dad as their best man before, but when he explained his reasons, I could understand. He had been his best mate his whole life through, and that is normally the person you chose. As I got to know Chris over the years, I knew why he meant so much to him; to now see the pain and fear in his face at the thought he may lose him was just horrendous. All I could do was be there for him and tell him how strong he was. He would fight this with every breath in body. Chris was a big, strong man who when he sang was a mixture of Tom Jones and Matt Munroe. If the reality shows were around when he was young, he would have won hands down. Barry just couldn't accept his beloved dad was not going to get better.

Chris steadily got worse as the weeks went by, and on 11 January 2003, we visited him in hospital as usual. He was his normal chirpy self, always had a smile on his face, laughing and joking with the nurses. Little did we know less than twelve hours later, Barry's mum, Rita, would call to say that we needed to get back to the hospital, that he didn't have long left. How had this happened so quickly? He was just a normal man going about his business, then on 18 December, his family's lives were turned upside down with this terrible news.

We were now being told we were about to lose him; we just couldn't take it in.

Barry and I raced to the Royal Hospital; the whole family sat with him until his last breath at 12.20 on 12 January. Barry's world came crashing down around him.

I watched as he clung to the man he adored, my own heart breaking at not being able to help ease his pain. This was only the fourth time I had seen him cry. The times before had been tears of joy at the birth of our boys. These were painful tears that came straight from the heart. Just like his dad, he is a big strong man. To see him fall at the loss of his father was just terrible to watch; how could he ever get over this loss?

I knew as a family, we could overcome anything; we would sit for hours, just talking about his dad. All the stories of Barry growing up is what helped him deal with the loss of the man he called God. Still to this day, I often see a little tear roll down his face when he hears a Tom Jones or Matt Monroe song or when he talks about the true gentleman he was and the fantastic father to his children.

Chapter 30

Life continued for us, always with a big black cloud of pain hanging over us at the loss of Chris, my own children bewildered at the loss of their granddad, my own mum commenting how sad she was to see them upset. Less than two months after Chris's death, the worst possible news was to hit my own family, with the devastating diagnosis of lung cancer to hit my beloved mum. She had been unwell for a while, but never in my wildest dreams did I think it would be cancer. That dreaded disease was going to destroy our family once again. Like Barry's dad, my mum was a strong woman who had been through so much in her life, even the loss of her first grandson. I really did believe in my heart she would recover.

I could never imagine my life without her; that picture was just too painful to think about.

It was only a couple of years before she had a triple heart bypass and got over it; we were convinced she was invincible.

The day she went in for the bypass, she wasn't worried about the operation. She wanted to get through it for her girls and grandchildren.

I knew this loving, caring woman who I had the privilege of calling Mum would not go without a fight. She gave me a letter that day and told me to open it after she had gone in to the theatre. I looked at the envelope. She named each one of us in the order of our birth, and in that letter, she was thanking each of us for bringing her so much joy and happiness, along with her grandchildren and sons-in-law, who she also adored, and they all adored her.

I still have that letter today; when I need her guidance or just the comfort of her touch, I will read it. I still feel that pain of losing her today as I did eleven years ago.

When I was growing up, I never thought I could love anyone the way I loved her, until my own children came along. Although I adored Barry, the love I felt for my mum and sons was immense. I now understood what it felt like to live your whole life for your kids.

Here I was, on 6 March 2003, sitting with the same doctor who had told us we were going to lose my father-in-law, but he was now telling us the news that our mum was about to leave her beloved girls.

I will never forget the pain that ran from my head to my toes when he said the words, 'She has three months to live'.

I felt like my heart was about to stop; I found myself cradling my elder sister Paula in my arms as her screams could be heard from all over the hospital.

I was trying to calm her down. I didn't want my mum to know what we had just been told. Her ward was across the hallway from his office, and if she heard the news we had just been told, she may have just given up. Even though in our hearts we knew she was aware of how long she had left, we tried to shield her as much as we could.

How was life ever going to be the same again, not just for me, but also my sisters and all the grandchildren as well as our dad? They had spent forty-four years together; the effect it would have on him would be soul destroying.

The thought of never again seeing that beautiful, smiling face was the hardest thing to imagine. I had seen first-hand what grief had done to Barry. Now I was faced with the same thing. The pain I felt was one I hadn't felt before.

That day is still so clear in my mind. We went to tell my dad the news. He was not well himself at the time. I knew the effect it would have on him. As much as they may have argued, we all knew she was his life. How were we going to break the news, the woman he met on a blind date all those years ago was about to leave his side?

Kathy sat him down and told him what the doctor had said. He stood up and walked upstairs. We all looked at each other, not knowing what to say.

My dad was a man of few words and always kept his emotions in check; the next minute, in he came with his suit and cap on. He wanted to hear the news from the doctor himself and felt he had to wear his suit for what he was about to hear.

An hour later, my dad walked back into the living room a broken man. He sat for a little while with his head in his hands. He had heard the news himself. This was now reality. He was losing his soul mate.

He told us that day, 'We have to be strong for your mother; she needs all of us'.

He knew each one of us would fall without her, so the seven of us made a pact that day: We would keep it together to make her time with us as memorable as possible and do everything we could to keep her with us for as long as we could.

My youngest sister Michelle searched the Internet for alternative cures. She was given everything organic from here on in. We were convinced this would help. She was so determined in her quest to help heal Mum, she devoted all her time to this. She also had chemotherapy; this was stopped, as it was making her worse.

She wanted one last memory with each of her girls and asked us all to spend time with her. She also wanted each of us to have the memory of our time with her.

When it was my day, she asked me to take her to New Brighton with all the kids. As she sat in the wheelchair, watching them play, my heart was breaking into tiny little pieces, thinking, *Will this be the last thing we do together?*

I have the most beautiful memories from a little girl going shopping with her and taking her on holiday with Barry and the kids. Every year, we went to Tenerife. The year she had her bypass, she couldn't fly, so we went to Butlins in Minehead for a week.

She was the happiest when she was with her grandchildren. She would look after all of them in the six-weeks holidays, just so we could work. Nothing was ever too much for her, and now the tears were falling, watching that beautiful smile etched upon her angel face, as she watched them all play.

Here I was, trying to cram in as many memories, storing them. I knew we were on borrowed time. On the outside, my smile was painted on just for her, but inside, my heart was falling apart.

Throughout her illness, she never once complained, nor did she think, *Why me?* With a strong spirit and the joy she carried right through life, she dealt with it as she had with the losses of Joseph and all her brothers and sisters: with strength, courage, and determination to keep fighting for her girls.

When that day came, I had just gone to bed, and my eldest sister rang.

I was not prepared for what I would be met with when I got to her house. As I ran up the stairs, the paramedics were working on her, and I knew from the look on her face, she was gone. We followed the ambulance to the hospital, knowing what news would be awaiting us. As we all walked in, we were ushered into the family room. You know when you go in there, the news is bad.

As the doctor walked in he then ran back out to get a nurse. As soon as he had seen all our faces, he said he panicked.

Those words the doctor delivered had now taken away every bit of hope we had. In the minutes after the news, all you could hear were the screams of each of us, our whole lives now destroyed in one sentence: 'Sorry, we couldn't do no more'.

How would I ever smile again? My mum, who had taught me how to love, who had shown me what passion was, who had displayed empathy for everyone she met, and most of all, her beautiful smile along with her character. Everyone would still say to this day how funny she was.

She had a knack of brightening up the darkest day. She could light a room up with her smile. How would my world go around without her in it?

I was lost for so long, I never thought I would be normal again. We still had to deliver the news to the grandchildren. She wasn't just their Nan, she was the mum to all of them as well as us. My own boys were still reeling from the loss of their granddad. Now they had lost the lynchpin of our family.

I remember thinking how doctors get it so right. My mum lasted three months and four days from when she was first diagnosed.

Our mum was there for every one of us. No matter how often we needed her, her life was put on hold from the day Kathy was born right through to the day she left. She was still thinking of us.

Looking back, I believe she knew she was going that day. She had had radium pumped right through her body to find out if the cancer had spread. She wasn't allowed around the children for twenty-four hours due to the after-effects, but that didn't stop her seeing them. She asked me would I bring them over and she would look at them out of the window. She wanted their faces to be fresh in her memory when she left us.

The funeral came, and my dad decided he couldn't go. I understood his reasons. I remember going into his room. He was sitting looking out of the window. His words were, 'Girl, I loved her. I can't watch her go down a hole', but I know in his mind, if he didn't see it, he could imagine she was still here. My heart broke even more at how lonely he would be without her. For all those years, they had shown their love for each other by arguing, so now she was gone, I worried what would happen to him.

Chapter 31

The weeks after my mum's death were just a blur. I would go to bed crying and wake up crying.

Some days just drinking to numb the pain. I had completely lost my way. She had not only shown me the importance of being the best mum you could be to your children if they are to thrive, but she had also shown me how to carry myself as a woman and what you want the world to see.

Now she was gone, I didn't see any point in going on, not even the thought of my babies kept me going.

I remember my friend Sandra coming into my bedroom and just crying when she looked at what I had become. Sandra and her sister Paula had been my friends since I was sixteen (and they are still my friends today).

I had watched them lose their beloved mum, Rosie, and knew the hurt they had gone through. The thought of going through that pain was too much to handle. There were seven of us from the age of twenty, who all started to have children. I was the only one who didn't have a daughter. Paula decided I was to be godmother to my beautiful Mollie. I don't feel like I have missed out, because I have always had her. She makes my birthdays so special and has done so since she could understand. I had always wanted the relationship my mum had with each of us. I don't just have this with all my sons, I also have it with my Mollie. She is everything I would have wanted in a girl.

The unthinkable happened four weeks after losing my mum: Barry had fallen fourteen feet from a roof he was working on and was lucky to be alive. It was only by luck he had put trainers on that day instead of his work boots; the doctor told us the way he had fallen normally causes the organs to shut down with shock. Someone was watching over him that day.

If ever I questioned fate and what exactly it had in store for us, I certainly did then.

I was due back into work the next day after being off from my mum's death. Here I was, now wondering how I was going to cope with this, although I do believe fate does play a part, because it was Barry's accident that pulled me back into reality and the realisation that I could so easily have lost my husband so soon after my mum and father-in-law.

I count ourselves lucky that Barry did live. One week after he had fallen, a man working on another site died after falling from the same height. Yes, his injuries were catastrophic, but he was alive.

He would be in a wheelchair for six months and had to rely on sticks to help him walk for two years after the accident. He still suffers from the effects of it to this day. Some days, he really struggles walking.

In all of the time he was in the hospital, he never once thought about himself and would try to convince me he wasn't in pain, all the time worrying about how I would cope. That was him all over, always putting me first, just like when he lost his idol. He did not want me to see him upset, still displaying his strength of character. Even with broken feet and in the height of pain, he wouldn't let it stop him being a dad or a husband.

This was the second accident he had in under twelve months. Just before he lost his dad, he had sliced right through his leg with a grinder. We always knew the job was dangerous, but Barry enjoyed it and it paid well. Now, we didn't even know if he would walk again, never mind work.

Chapter 32

After I found out I would lose my mum, we decided to look at emigrating to Australia. We had friends in Brisbane who had been asking us to visit for a long time and had already paid for a holiday the following September to help us make the final decision.

I knew I would find it difficult to get over my mum, so moving to Australia, I believed, I could have accepted it more, and after all that had happened, we were actually looking forward to the holiday to try and help us come to terms with events of the past year.

I now had to deliver the news to the boys their holiday they had been looking forward to was not going to happen.

In seven months, they had lost their granddad and their nan, and now their dad was lying in a hospital bed. Not knowing what news was coming next, it got to the point where I became quite angry and questioned what we had done to deserve all this in such a short space of time. Kids being kids, they didn't really understand the magnitude of what was happening, and all they kept saying was what they would miss out on, not realising at the time they were lucky to have a dad. I look back on these difficult times, just as I often do when I was a little girl, and these moments are what have helped shape me into the person I have become.

That phone call I got on the Thursday afternoon from Barry to go and pick him up, telling me he had broken his feet, to me thinking he was exaggerating because he was so calm, little did I know how bad he really was.

We had to swop roles after Barry came home from hospital. He couldn't work for five years after the accident, due to the operations he had and the pain he endured just walking. Like everything else, we got through it together. I was still working, sometimes up to sixty hours per week, to ensure the kids didn't go without. Barry looked after the house as best he could. Michelle would often help out with Barry and the house, even though she was still reeling from the death of Mum. I do often wonder how we made it through that year, but somehow we did, and it just made us stronger.

Chapter 33

My friend whom I had trained to become an agent only a couple of years before had decided to move to Spain and had been talking to me about it. Thinking of the money we had saved with not going to Australia, I spoke to Barry, and we made a decision the kids needed a new start as well as us. We chose to give it a go and look first. Although I still had my dad and Barry had his mum, we felt the kids would benefit from a fresh start. We decided to go and look at houses the following November. We needed something positive to cling to, and this would bring excitement back for my boys as well as be a distraction for us after what we had been through.

Even though I was scared, I knew this would be good for us as a family to just be normal, people not knowing what we had gone through in the last twelve months, positive steps for the kids; also, Barry really needed a holiday after the accident.

That big, strong man had shown himself more than ever. He was dealing with the death of his father and an accident that would leave him disabled for life, and he was worried about me losing my mum.

In our eighteen years together, he had seen first-hand what my love for my mum was, and that is the reason he wanted to love and care for me so much, to help me come to terms with it.

In November 2003, we set off for a two-week holiday to Spain to look for our dream home; after searching for three days, we settled on a lovely little place called Ciudad Quesada. This was to become our home for nearly two years.

I had been in my present role for three years by now and was finding it really difficult to concentrate after the year's events. I would often find myself thinking how different my life had been twelve months ago, how happy I had been. The difference a year can make is unreal.

After purchasing the house, I informed my boss I would be leaving the following year, as the house wouldn't be ready until the following August. This would give us time to save as much up as possible as well as sell our own house.

Chapter 34

The year was about to end as it started, with more devastating news, which would have a huge impact on my work life as well as my home life.

On 4 December, we found ourselves with the heartbreaking news that our dad may not last the night. On arrival to the Royal Hospital, he was rushed into resuscitation; the doctor on duty informed us, 'Your dad is a very sick man with severe pneumonia. He will not last the night'. He asked us did we want him made comfortable and let nature take its course, or he could go to intensive care, where he would probably die anyway. We all looked at each other, thinking the same thoughts.

I remember feeling quite upset that a doctor could even suggest this. Of course, we would do everything in our power to keep him. We hadn't even gone six months without our mum, and now this doctor is telling us we are about to lose my dad. I still often wonder what reaction this doctor would have had if someone had that same conversation with him he had with us.

That decision was easy; he was going to intensive care. We had to take that chance. Even with what the doctor had told us, it wasn't fair to just leave him to die. We also knew if anyone could fight, it was him.

He was a slightly built man but had the strength of an ox, so we were prepared to bet on him waking up.

I knew deep down from the conversation I had with him on the day of my mum's funeral, he would find it hard to be here without her, but I also believe he didn't want to die.

I remember standing in resuscitation staring at him, thinking how I had never really got to know him. He may have been my dad, and I loved him, but I could never see past my mum. Now I regretted that and decided there and then, if he pulls through, I would build the relationship we had never had and get to know him the way my sisters had. If I could have changed anything, it would have been the relationship between myself and my dad.

He was taken up to intensive care around 6.30 that evening.

The doctor came to see us and advised us they were making him comfortable; we would be able to see him in a few hours. Dr Marx came out at 10.30 that evening and told us he wouldn't last the night. He advised all relatives to say their goodbyes.

His brothers and sisters came in. I watched as they all stood in shock at the thought of losing their big brother. He was a hero to them. At seventeen, he signed my nan's signature to pass for the army, and off he went to the Korean War. He went there as a boy and came back a man.

He was an inspiration to them. He survived that war and saw some terrible atrocities, the worst being in between two comrades shot dead. The only time he ever spoke about the war was when he had a drink. We never really knew what damage it did to him. Looking back, I wonder how he carried those images right though out his life without any help to get over it.

The room was packed with family members wanting to say their goodbyes. My uncle Michael stood there just shaking his head, not really knowing what to do or say. He was just like him, a strong confident man, who I looked up to so much. He was the one who had played a part in our lives growing up, and the very first car I ever went in was his. The stories he would tell us would have us all laughing, and now I was watching the bewilderment and sadness etched upon his face.

As the night wore on and the extended family went home, we tried to get as comfortable as possible, taking turns to sit with him. As the hours were passing, we dared to hope the doctors got it wrong this time.

I spent as much time as I could at his bedside. I thought it was the least I could do. After all, I hadn't given him much time when he was well, so I wanted to spend his last few hours with him holding his hands. My sisters joked if he had woken up and seen who was holding his hand, he would have collapsed there and then. We still tried to laugh, even through the unimaginable pain we were going through. Humour is what got us through all the difficult times, even as kids growing up with so little, and now was no different.

It went into the early hours, and he was still here; in came Dr Marx at 5.20 a.m. He couldn't believe we were still in the waiting room. His actual words were, 'Your dad must be a very strong man to last this long'. The pneumonia was classed as the worst case it can be.

I will always remember that doctor and all that he done for my dad whilst he was in the intensive care. He was a soft-spoken man with a very gentle face and made for this profession. The compassion he showed us as a family was second to none.

My dad's condition didn't improve over the coming days, but he was still fighting. We had now been told to go hour by hour. As the clock ticked, we would be waiting for the next hour to pass, hoping against hope it would continue. The doctors and nurses couldn't understand how this man who barely weighed eight stone was still with us three days after being told he wouldn't last the night. In real terms, he should have died in the resuscitation unit. No one had bargained what this great man had been through and overcome, so pneumonia wasn't going to take him.

We started to believe he was over the worst, as he had now lasted five days, but that hope was short-lived when Dr Marx came to tell us it really was only a matter of time. By now, his liver was failing, and once that went, it would be the end of the road and all our hopes gone. He then told us about a trial drug that had only been used before in Scotland, and this could help repair his liver. My dad was going to be a guinea pig. We decided to vote as a family on whether he should have it or not, because of the possible complications that came with it. I decided against it, because I felt like he had been through enough and didn't want him to suffer any more. I am so glad that more people voted to try it than voted against it. That drug was the turning point for him.

Six weeks after that awful day, my dad was now strong enough to go to the high dependency unit. He was sitting up and talking. We thought maybe our luck was changing, and I had more time to get to know him now he was awake.

I had decided to give up my job when my dad became so ill. I knew I was needed in the hospital. I wouldn't be able to commit the hours so felt it only fair to resign.

In March of that year, he was moved to a ward where, at the time, MRSA was rife, and we had been advised to keep an eye on him.

We still took it in turns to sit with him; he had come so far and was now looking like his old self. He had not had fresh air since December and asked me could I take him to the front of the hospital. With the doctor's permission, off we went.

As I had promised myself, I started to build my relationship with him. He would often comment on how much I looked like my mum. We both had very strong personalities, and this is the reason we clashed when I was growing up.

I was always the one who answered back, disobeyed, and questioned everything, so looking back, I understood why he got annoyed with me. That was the first and last time he would get to go to the front of the hospital. I am so glad it was me who took him. That day meant so much to me. We just talked about stuff that I didn't think he was interested in and about how much he missed my mum.

Well, my dad's health started to decline rapidly. Despite all the hard work of Dr Marx and his team, he was now failing again. We were now being told he had MRSA, so we knew the end was coming. The mention of that brought terror to anyone in hospital.

He was transferred to Broadgreen Hospital. Nearly five months after being told he wouldn't last the night, his body had finally taken enough, and he closed his eyes forever. It wasn't even twelve months since we had lost my mum, and now we were burying him. It was also five days before what would have been their first anniversary apart in forty-four years; he was now joining her.

I still say it was the right decision to take him to intensive care that day. In those five months, I got to know my dad, and he went to sleep knowing I really did love him.

I was the only one out of the six of us whose love he questioned. I thank God he pulled through on that fateful day, enough for us to mend our broken relationship.

The weeks after the loss of my dad, I was just going on auto pilot. I hadn't even come to terms with my mum's death, now I was grieving for my dad. I also knew I was not going to let my own family down this time and decided the house was going up for sale, and we were going to Spain sooner rather than later.

Chapter 35

We really needed some positive energy after the events of the last sixteen months, so moving and making a new start is what we needed as a family. Although I felt guilty leaving my sisters and their families, I believed at the time that a change was necessary for mine. We had all lost so much, but my kids had also suffered the loss of their granddad and were lucky to have a dad. I needed to make the change for them.

We set off on our adventure on 17 August 2004, hoping above hope we could leave all the heartache behind us and be happy.

Spain was to be a mixture of emotions, from getting lost in France on our way, to playing tennis on the lawn using the clothes maiden as a net.

It was the first time in nearly two years I had laughed so much my belly hurt; that is when I knew we would be okay.

I never thought after losing my mum I would laugh again, and here I was laughing so much because I saw myself in Christopher that day. When he threw the racket because I was beating him, it took me back to those precious memories in the caravan when I first tipped the board up because I was getting beaten.

He was displaying that same hunger to win and disappointment when he didn't. I realised once again, when you are backed into a corner, whether it's personal or work life, that fighting spirit will show itself, and at that time, I don't think I could have displayed more fighting spirit just to be where we were. That day proved I had tons of it.

When we left Liverpool to drive to Spain, my final stop was the cemetery to say goodbye to my mum and dad in my own way and somehow let them know where we were going. My kids were so excited to start this new chapter in our lives.

When I look back at the most difficult time I had ever gone through, I strongly believe there is a lesson to be learnt from it all. My belief is they happen at a time in our lives to help shape what we become as people. At the worst times, we can go one of two ways.

I was a certain type. No matter what life throws my way, I will come back stronger, wiser, and thankful, that little girl growing up with the most loving mum a girl could wish for, to sharing clothes and building unbreakable bonds with my five sisters, as well as starting out in a one-bedroom flat, to now making a new life for our family displays the character I was born with.

During that journey, we went through every emotion possible. We tried to put in perspective what we had been through and why. We talked and reminisced; we laughed and we cried at what we had lost; and we got excited at the future. We had a whole new beginning, and we were going to make the most of it.

By now, the boys were getting older. Christopher was coming up to fifteen, Leighton was eleven, and Joseph coming up to ten. They were old enough to enjoy the experience of driving through France in every single weather forecast, from sleet and great big hailstones, to thunder and lightning and rain, then finally the sun. The worst part was driving through thunder and lightning and not a hotel in sight. We drove for hours, Kathy back home Googling all the whereabouts of hotels, in the end praying. Finally, after driving for hours, we came to a hotel. It was like the Star of David, all lit up in the night sky. The relief we felt was unreal.

After driving for nearly thirty-six hours, we finally arrived in our new home. When we saw the sign for Ciudad Quesada, we jumped for joy. Our excitement in the car couldn't be contained.

Chapter 36

As with all the trials and tribulations we had been through, Spain came with a whole new set of challenges. We weren't sure what we would do workwise. Barry still could not walk properly, never mind work, but we had quite a bit of money from the sale of the house, which would buy time for us to decide what we wanted to do.

After a few months of relaxing, we decided to open a fish and chip shop. As there wasn't one close by, we thought it was a great idea. When working at my previous job, I used to have lunch from a place called the Big Chippy, so that was to be the name of the new business.

The shop we chose was a shell, and we started work on it the following March. We had to build it from scratch. I went from putting in false ceilings, to helping tiling and erecting stairs, ready for an Internet café at a later date.

This project lasted until the September of that year, and every hurdle that could have been placed in our way was. Finally realising it wasn't meant to be and with heavy hearts, we decided to walk away.

We had put so much into this venture. The bulk of our savings were quickly disappearing. The decision had to be made whilst we still had a little left. Also, our marriage was now being affected, and I was not prepared to go through all what had happened and then come to Spain to split up. That for me would have been a travesty. Yes, we had lost all that we had worked our whole lives for in that shop, but we still had our health and each other. Losing the money was nothing compared to what we could have lost, as well as what we had already lost. This put things in perspective for us.

My motto is when doors open for us, not all of them have what we want behind them. Sometimes, we may walk through one, to find we have to turn around and walk back out. That doesn't mean we don't learn from going through theses doors, it just means whatever was there wasn't for us. I learned I can make a decision which was very difficult, but it was also the right one for us at the time.

By November of that year, Paula and Marie had to pay the mortgage. We now couldn't afford the repayments, and we were talking about coming home. At this point, I didn't feel like we had failed, it was more of a life's lesson, and it also helped me come to terms with my mum's loss. Although I did feel bad, I had taken my family from everything they had known to a strange country, with the hope that we would have a better life. Here, we now were not even able to pay the mortgage, so I did feel I had let them down.

It really was only a matter of time before we would be going home. I remember sitting on the balcony of the house, talking with Barry and crying, thinking how fifteen months before, when driving to Spain, we had so many dreams and expectations of what our future was going to be, and now we were talking about going home. Barry was his usual supportive self, telling me we couldn't know what would happen. Life is for learning. We definitely learnt from Spain.

At that time, I also knew whatever decision we made, it would all turn out well. What I had taken from our time in Spain was the friendships we made there as well as our cocker spaniel dog, Clio. We bought when we first arrived.

Clio was the best thing we could have bought for the boys.

The decision to go home was made for us on November 5, when my brother-in-law rang to hit us with more bad news. My uncle Michael, who I loved so much, had passed away. I thought of all the lovely memories I had of him when I was a child and he would visit us. God, I was wondering when all this bad news was going to stop; it just seemed to keep coming at us.

It was decided I would fly home on the Monday and Barry would follow a week later with the boys. We only had enough for one flight, and the prices the following week were cheaper.

We were so grateful for friends we had met in Spain who gave Barry the money to fly home, not knowing when we would pay them back. They had shown such kindness and compassion in our time of need. We also didn't have the money to bring Clio home, as it was so expensive to put her through the quarantine. We had to make another difficult decision to leave her there. This was harder than losing all our money in the business. This little tiny dog had done so much for us as a family. What would we do without her? She had taken away the grief I had so often seen in my children's eyes, that was now replaced with laughter from Clio's antics. I didn't know how we were going to break the news to them.

After sitting them down and explaining the situation, they all informed us they were okay with leaving her there for now, because they knew it was temporary and we would soon have her back. I remember praying whilst I was talking to them that we would get her back. At the time, I honestly didn't know whether we would. In the last two years, the hand we had been dealt was making me question my faith, but I did believe in my heart she would be coming home in the future, just so I could once again see the laughter in their eyes.

The day I walked out of our house in Spain to fly home to the news of losing my uncle, who had been my hero from a child, this alone was hard enough to deal with. I also had to look for a house for us, as well as try and secure my old job back. All of this as well as leaving Barry and my boys, on top of not knowing whether I would ever see my little Clio again, was just too much to take, and I just literally broke down in the airport. Again, I knew it had to be done. I do believe we are only ever given what God knows we can deal with, but I felt like we had been given more than our fair share. Surely new doors would start opening for us.

That flight home, knowing what awaited me, as well as what I had to do, was all I could think of. That had to be the longest flight of my life. It was also on that flight that I knew our time in Spain was done. It had served its purpose, even if it was at a huge cost, although over the years, I have often wondered how our lives would have turned out if we had made the decision to stay. I had that same feeling in my gut I had felt so many times before, knowing things have a way of sorting themselves out.

Chapter 37

The Tuesday after arriving home, I had arranged to meet my old boss about my previous job. He was the regional manager at the time and a man I have always held in high regard; he was not only very good at his job, but his people skills were second to none. He would play a big part throughout my career, and my respect for him just grew. He went on to become the H/R manager, and whenever I needed support or advice, he was always there to offer it.

He was fantastic at knowing what to say, and I learned so much from working under his leadership, as well as when he changed roles. He was the first manager that I aspired to be. The role of an H/R manager became available, and I applied for it, thinking how lucky I would be to work alongside him and learn from him. Although I never got the job, he carried on teaching me and advising me over the years. He was also the first person who taught me how to be articulate.

I got my job back and recall saying to Barry, how on the day we left for Spain I felt like my time at this company wasn't done. Now here I was right back where I had first learnt how to be a manager. As well as knowing when I am done with something and it's time to walk away, I also know when I haven't finished with something. I still had the area manager role to think of. Sometimes we may get side-tracked from our path, but our eventual journey will always lead back to that path to finish what we first started.

Chapter 38

After the excitement of getting my job back and setting my sights on the area manager role, Barry was still unable to work due to him needing further operations on his feet.

I still had to find us a home. Although it would be easier to rent now I had a job, I had to first find one. I was staying with Michelle for the week I was home alone and found it really hard without Barry and the kids.

I spent the week looking at lots of houses all over Liverpool. Not one of them felt like home.

The following week, Barry arrived home with the kids. Even though we still didn't have a house they were home, so that made it a little easier.

For the next two weeks, we had to split up as a family. Barry and I stayed with our friends Dave and Sharon in Wales, and the kids stayed with Tricia. Whilst we were there, our friend advised us his brother had offered his house in Widnes for us to stay until we found somewhere. Although it was away from friends and family, it wasn't as far as Spain, and we were grateful to have a home. We would all be back together as a family.

I did question how we had got to this point; with no furniture, we had to buy all our kitchen utensils from Asda for less than £20.

I had grown up with very little and as an adult had worked hard to have all the things my mum and dad could have only dreamt of. Now, I was back to being that little girl again with nothing to call our own, but again I believe this was all part of the picture, proving once again no matter what you go through, with a positive and optimistic outlook and action, you can overcome anything.

I had now faced adversity so many times, I was not about to give up now. What I lacked in height I more than made up for with determination and strength of character to keep going.

Chapter 39

On my first day back in work, I made a decision that it was now time to concentrate on achieving my goal of becoming an area manager and I would ensure I stood out for what I was good at, which was training and developing individuals as well as getting results. I enjoyed this part of the role so much. My greatest pleasure was always helping others exceed their own expectations and my reason for my now new chosen career.

After being back only three months, I was called into the area manager's office and advised I would be moving to the sister company in another office, due to the relocation of another manager. Because I was only back on a temporary contract, I was the one who had to make way for the manager.

I was absolutely devastated to be leaving the branch where I had learnt the tricks of the trade. This meant not only a new area manager but also a new regional manager, and my agents had become friends. I was leaving them behind; although I had to accept it, there wasn't much I could do. I was also excited at the new challenges ahead. Although it was the sister company and they all worked under the same umbrella, they had a completely different way of working, and I was excited at the thought of a new way of learning. Looking back, this move was a turning point in my career.

Any doubts or worries I may have had at the thought of a new office were all gone on the first day. I was made to feel part of that team, as though I had always been there. Although I was sad to leave my previous branch, and I had a new set of colleagues as well as a whole new set of agents, this was the branch I enjoyed most as a development manager. It also came with more trials that would challenge me as a manager. For every trial, tribulation, and challenge I have faced (not just in my career, but also my personal life), I have always learnt as well as grown from it.

The long days had to continue if I were to get anywhere close to my goal of area manager. I felt it necessary to show improvements in the section and get results if I was to stand out and achieve the ultimate.

As with my previous agents, I guided and advised them of what to look for when improving their agencies. This would give them more knowledge and improve their own capabilities. Also, teaching them to believe in themselves was so important if they were to continue getting the results and earning commissions from their agencies.

After being at my new branch for a number of months, there was talk of redundancies, and because I was still temporary, I felt I would be the first to go. I now had also moved back to Liverpool, after renting in Widnes for six months, we decided we would buy a new build, again I was determined to get back on the property ladder. I then decided I would apply for a permanent position in the Liverpool city centre branch, where I had started out as an agent all those years ago and where my desire to become an area manager had first started.

Chapter 40

I got the job and started there in September 2006, and just like the previous branches I had worked in, there were problems on the section I was to take over. As much as I was apprehensive, I was also now ready to prove a point. I had grown as person from the one who stood in his office all those years ago. I had taken his advice on board and was now ready to start my journey towards fulfilling my dream.

I had decided this was to be the branch in which I would be promoted from. Nothing was going to stand in my way. Those words are what had pushed me on over the years, and here I was, in the branch that I was so desperate to be part of.

I was given Halewood and Garston to manage. The sections had huge problems and two vacancies, one of which had been vacant for two years. I still remember that agency number to this day. It was of such poor quality, I was surprised it stayed open. My first priority was to fill the vacancies and ensure the new agents were trained to the highest standard to help them achieve top commissions, ensuring they would stay. I knew I had my work cut out. I also knew I would succeed.

The first thing I did was work on that agency to improve the quality of the book, to guarantee a new agent a decent commission base to build on, as well as ensuring I was still providing support for the other agents. These agents were weary of me. They had seen so many managers coming and going, promising them the world and then leaving before anything came to fruition.

I knew what you could achieve as an agent if you were provided support and a direction. I was determined to give them what they needed, along with the wisdom to improve their own capabilities.

I can honestly say they gave me everything back in return for what I did for them. When I was leaving, one agent said she would not be telling her customers I had left; this would stop them paying, which was a lovely compliment.

I didn't just build relationships with my agents, I also built that same rapport with the customers. I could relate to some of the situations they found themselves in and was able to empathise with them, so I would put a payment plan in place that would suit everyone involved, although it wasn't always that easy. The job of collecting money can be risky, and some customers would sometimes threaten you. I would always act professional and walk away from these situations. I knew it was never personal. Sometimes, people act out when they are desperate.

Six months after arriving, I had filled both vacancies. The results were so good, we had taken the section from the bottom of the company to number one in the region. I had done what I set out to do.

I stood out for all the right reasons. I had my agents to thank for all their hard work since I arrived. Everything I taught them, they would go out and put it in place. The question now was keeping it there. I would constantly be educating myself in how to lead teams and empower them. I was regularly researching great leaders and learning about what practices they put in place. I wasn't just educating myself on a regular basis, I was doing the same with my agents.

My saying has always been to never give less than 100 percent in everything you do, whether that has been cleaning my house, being a mum, or in my career, and I instilled this in every agent I worked with.

A lot of my agents were older than I was, but they always displayed respect for me, because I had not only been in their shoes, I had also treated them as I would wish to be treated myself, with total respect and integrity. I depended on their support in turning the section around.

This was a city branch and came with a lot more complex problems, and this is where I grew more, both as a manager and an individual. I was using skills I didn't even know I had. Just to keep bums on seats was hard enough, but that wasn't ever enough for me.

I always wanted to bring the best out in people and help them be the best version of themselves, and that was the reason I educated myself to ensure my section was always going to be at the top. If my agents were earning top commission, they were happy. I ensured my support for them was never compromised.

These agents had only ever been used to attending meetings in order to be told they were the bottom of the region. They were now in the top position in the region. I believe what contributed to their continued success was that they were now being praised for their hard work instead of given a dressing-down about their commitment. The morale on the section was at an all-time high at the sense of achievement from them all. I was so proud to play a part in it.

In October and November of that year, the branch made its bonus for the first time in nine months. The work I completed in the three months I had been there had such an impact on the figures, and this was because of the time and effort I had put in.

I will also never forget that first Christmas in the branch. We had a promotion on, and if you achieved the customer count for the section, you received a large sack of chocolates. I was the only one not to receive the chocolates and that is when I realised the team spirit within that branch was not there amongst the managers. Bearing in mind my contribution had secured a bonus for two months in a row, they seemed to forget this. I remember being upset at the time but decided I would take something positive from this and try to build that spirit within the team.

I often joked with my manager at the time, how his words all those years ago had played a huge part in my desire to become a manager. If ever I felt like giving up, I would draw on that conversation to keep me focused.

I knew my goal was in sight. I hadn't just turned one section around, but three, and all in different locations, coming up against different issues in each location. I was becoming wiser and more confident in my role. This was now boosting my credibility with my manager and the regional manager.

Chapter 41

Nineteen months after starting in this branch, my manager rang me one Monday morning to ask if I would take over the branch, as he would be off for a little while. I was in complete shock to get that call. I was third in line for this, being the last manager to start at the branch.

I remember being so excited at the time, I couldn't even talk, and then reality struck me. Oh my goodness, this was finally real; after all those years of dreaming, I was now being given the chance to see if I was good enough.

I was also quite nervous and questioning my own ability now. I knew this was the most difficult branch in the region, and if I was to fail, it would have been here. I knew I had a job and a half, but the way I looked at it, it may only be for a couple of weeks, so I was thinking it will just be to report figures. I didn't really see myself as the area manager at this point.

Richard Branson once said, 'If you are offered an opportunity and can't do it, accept and learn later', and that is what I did.

But I knew if it was longer, my role was going to change, and I would have to earn the respect of my colleagues whom I had worked alongside for the last nineteen months. A couple of these managers had been appointed as the person in charge when the manager went on holiday. I really needed to display the strength of character needed to fill this role.

I lay awake all night, talking it over with Barry and thinking of the negatives, trying to talk myself out of what could be the biggest opportunity of my life. Failure was now at the forefront of my mind and letting the regional manager down. This made the decision harder for me.

When I woke up, I still didn't have the answer. What I did know is this is what I had worked my whole life for, to prove I had the capabilities to be successful in the role. The only regret I had was my mum and dad were not here to see this. Even though it was only temporary and I didn't know how long it would be for, I was so grateful to the regional manager for having faith in me.

My dream to finally reach my goal was within sight. I thought back to the days when I very nearly walked away because of rejection. That determination to carry on is what paid off in the end.

From a little girl, both my parents would often remark how much determination I displayed when I wanted something. They said you could see it in my eyes. I was also doing this to show to my sons how, no matter where you start in life, the world is yours for the taking if you work at it.

Chapter 42

My first day sitting in the area manager's chair felt surreal. I will never forget that sense of achievement. Even if I didn't go any further than that chair, the feeling I had inside, I had never felt in my career before.

I finally sat in the chair I had promised myself I would over ten years previously. Another lesson I learned that day is that when you are passionate about something and you set yourself a goal, as well as work hard, you will not lose.

But as excited as I was, my emotions were all over the place, worrying how difficult the job ahead would be and questioning my own ability. These thoughts soon disappeared when the regional manager came in and informed me he believed in me, and I should believe in myself. He also reminded me of all that I had already achieved and overcome since working under his leadership.

Six months before, I had been out collecting in a part of Liverpool that was known for gangs. As I was turning my car around, I could see out of the corner of my eye the end of a gun pointing at my head.

That was the one time I genuinely feared for my life. I will never forget the vision I could see in my mind's eye. They say your life flashes before you, and mine did. My boys, Barry, and my sisters and their families flashed right before my very eyes.

I thought I was never going to see them again. The thought of not watching them grow up and be part of their futures was just too painful to imagine. Not being able to influence any decisions they made or advise them was just incomprehensible. What seemed like hours was more like seconds. The thought of not being around when they needed a mum was something that affected me not just then, but months later. When you become so close to death, your whole outlook on life changes, and you as person change how you view the world.

My life had been so normal that day, leaving for work, starting the day as I still do to this day, telling my boys I love them. I thought I would never get to say those words again. My day has always started and ended with those important words.

I have always believed when children know they are loved and are encouraged in life, they can go on to achieve great things. I was thinking of how they would have missed out if that trigger had been pulled that day.

I remember the police turning up in bulletproof vests, and I was thinking what a waste of money. I hadn't been hurt physically, but mentally, I didn't know how I would be affected.

When I look back at that incident, the man was laughing as he held the gun to my head through the open window. He was probably laughing at the face I was pulling; the shock was unreal. I had found myself looking down the barrel of a gun. It was a really hot day, and I recall thinking, *Why did I have that window open?*

As the realisation sunk in at what had happened, I was so angry that this person thought he could pull a gun on me and walk away scot-free.

I put myself in even more danger and jumped out of the car, screaming like a wailing banshee, 'Who do you think you are?'

That was the feistiness in me to not let anyone get away with anything. That is the one thing I regret doing, as this could have had devastating consequences. It's a wonder he didn't shoot me to shut me up. I was like a lunatic.

With all the noise, people came running out of their houses. Someone advised me to call the police, otherwise I probably would have done exactly as I have always done and put it to the back of my mind. It was only then did I realise the seriousness of the situation. Another lesson I learned was to never underestimate what can happen, as well as never leave yourself open to get hurt. That taught me to always be security conscious.

When the police did arrive, they came in their droves, and I kept apologising for wasting their time. Just then, an officer informed me a man in the south of England had been killed with BB gun the week before; that sent shivers through me. All this had happened because I was helping out a new colleague who had three books to collect, and I had offered my services before starting my own work. That's when the severity hit me. If it wasn't so serious, it would have been quite funny.

When the police were taking a statement, they asked what kind of gun it was; because I am not familiar with them, just came out with, 'I think it may have been a bazooka'.

Barry looked at me in amazement. The policeman tried his best not to laugh, and I wondered why they were looking at me strange. He then asked me how big it was and what it looked like (he probably thought I was a crackpot). When I explained the size and description, he did laugh and said, 'Well, it definitely wasn't a bazooka'.

Barry was now hysterical, saying, 'What, was he going to shoot you with a bubble gum?' When I was a kid, we would buy Bazooka chewing gum and see who could make the biggest bubbles out of the gum. You could end up with pink gum all over your face if you blew one too big.

So the following year for my birthday, Barry (being his humorous self) bought me a whole box of Bazooka gum. He knew I would make light of it, as this is how I have always faced adversity. Humour is what has got me through all the ups and downs in the years before. Also, I was never going to be a victim, and if I let this affect me, then in my mind, I would have been just that.

I just classed it as another obstacle to overcome. I was still here to tell the tale, so no real damage was done.

That should really have put me off the job, but nothing was standing in my way of getting the area manager role, not even the little issue of a gun. I didn't want to make a big deal of it, just in case I looked weak. I took a couple of days off to collect my thoughts and spent them in Camelot with a friend and my boys. I have always believed if you sit thinking about past events, it will affect your future; my motto was to move on and learn from it.

The police didn't get the lad who done this to me. He had gone over all the back fences and through the estate. They stood no chance of catching him.

For every event or challenge that we face comes learning and growth, and this was no different. This was also what my regional manager was referring to when he explained he had the belief in me to succeed. He had seen first-hand how I dealt with trauma.

Chapter 43

I knew that day I wasn't going to fail. Although I don't like letting myself down, even more so, I don't like letting people down who have faith in me.

He taught me how to be a successful area manager and how you build great teams. Even though I had that cheekiness and steeliness about me and the will to win, he taught me the professional side of the business and how to earn the respect of your team. This was important if you were to get results. If you didn't earn respect in the job I was doing, you wouldn't be successful.

I wanted individuals to want to do well, not just for me, but more so for themselves. Yes, you got results by building great teams, but it was also important that I displayed the same sort of respect for the managers as I expected from them.

I have never been shy of hard work and supported my managers and agents. They repaid that by the results they delivered. The way in which he taught me was to always work towards others' strengths and not their weaknesses. This would build confidence from within and help them where they needed developing. This is exactly what he had done with me.

He knew I was a hard worker and I always got results, but he also knew what my weakness was, and that was the business side, so he started on teaching me everything that I would put into practise years later. He knew he could teach me this side; my mind was like a sponge. I absorbed everything I was taught and followed it to the letter and would utilise it when needed.

Because I didn't really understand at the time the importance of being professional and business minded, I would get infuriated with people and the excuses they came up with of why they had missed a budget. Sometimes, as he put it, I would ''open my gob before putting my brain into gear'. He taught me how to manage individuals in a different way, instead of being intolerant, give them a chance to explain what they would do differently.

By listening and watching him manage his team, I learnt how to become a more rounded and knowledgeable manager. This is what would bring me future success. I was always an impatient person until he taught me that with patience, you can teach people how to become great at anything they do.

Although he was a very good teacher, he did not suffer fools easily. He was always very tough when it came to results. If I didn't get targets for the week, I would have to provide him with a running commentary on what I had put in place and why it hadn't worked, as well as what I was doing differently to ensure results the following week.

I learnt very quickly I had to know my stuff and to try my best not to give bad results. I understood why he was strong. He had given me an opportunity to prove my worth. Also, it was the toughest in his region, so he needed to know I could step up to the plate.

That day, he informed me I would be acting manager for two weeks and then he would let me know if my manager would be returning. The two weeks flew by, and although performance still wasn't improving, I had started laying the foundations towards improvements, so he could see it would only be a matter of time.

Two weeks later, he came back in to advise me it would be a further four weeks, and he would ensure I got extra pay in my salary. My answer to that, because I wasn't well educated at the time and considered myself lucky he had put me in place, was, 'That's okay, I am enjoying the experience I am getting, even though it was much tougher than I had ever imagined'.

His reply was, 'Well, you might as well do it voluntary, and I'll have your salary'. Although it was condescending at the time, looking back, that was the naivety of me. No one would take on that extra work for no extra pay.

When I got my pay slip four weeks later and saw the extra income in my salary, that made me even more determined to step up. It was well worth the extra responsibility; from that moment on, I made sure I went over and beyond, as I was so grateful. I was able to spend it on the kids. Only having one wage coming in, the extra money was so important to us as a family.

Imagine my surprise when he came back in to tell me I would be staying as interim manager for a further six weeks and my salary would be going up by ten thousand pounds for the year, based on how long I would be in place.

I had to pretend to act normal, but inside I was screaming and working out in my head how much extra I would receive each month. Even if it was only another month, that money was going to do so much. I would have done well on the programme *Poker Face*; at the time, my expression was as if I was being offered this every day, but I didn't want to come across that the extra money was all I was after. What I lacked in business mind, I more than made up for in ambition, and he knew this.

What happened next was hilarious. I still shudder to this day at how embarrassed I was. I had acted so normal on hearing I would get the extra cash in my salary, but as soon as I left the room, I rang Barry to tell him the news.

I forgot where I was and just as all those years before when I displayed the excitement at wearing clothes from Next, I done exactly the same to Barry. I was that excited I couldn't get it out quick enough.

I turned around to find the Rom standing there laughing and telling me to be quiet, as everyone could hear my business. I wanted the floor to swallow me up at the humiliation I felt, but he then brought the managers in to inform them of my position for the foreseeable future, and I can honestly say, throughout my time as interim, every one of them displayed respect for me and worked hard to improve results in the area.

The next big step for me was to attend my first regional meeting. This meant I really was an area manager. I had always wondered what went on in these meetings. This is where I started to build up my business acumen.

From attending them and working alongside some of the best managers in the business, I started to understand it more and would go back to the branch full of energy and new ideas of what to improve. This is also where I built my confidence. Even though before, I had developed not just agents but also customers in how to conduct their accounts, I never really thought how I had done it before. By attending these meetings, I was learning what I had done to make things happen. I was becoming more conscious of what skills I would need when conducting specific duties.

I would just listen and observe the managers in the room. There was so much experience in there. I wanted to take every little bit I picked up and bottle it all in case I forgot anything. Anyone who knows me will tell you that this is a job in itself, as I have always done more talking than listening. But he also taught me that we have one mouth and two ears, so we must always listen twice as hard as we talk. I didn't always take that advice on board. I am a natural talker, although I do listen when necessary.

This is also where I built on my knowledge of how important team spirit and morale were. Over the years, I have worked in a lot of regions, some good and some not so good, but none of them compared to that first region where I learnt the ropes of the area manager. Their respect for each other was second to none, along with the tolerance to work together as a team, not just for the Rom, but also the Rom towards his team, and that is why it was so successful. They had a great teacher who not only guided them but gave them praise in a job well done.

Chapter 44

In my ten months as interim manager, I moved so far in my own capabilities that I now knew the role was definitely for me. Going back to the development manager role would be so hard. I had not just gotten used to the increase in salary but also the responsibility and the buzz I got from seeing regular improvements.

In the January before vacating the interim role, three area manager positions came up, covering Manchester South, Blackburn, and Bolton. Because I had done so well in Liverpool, I automatically thought I would stand the best chance. Wasn't I disappointed when I didn't get any of them? Another lesson I learned was to never assume anything.

I was interviewed by the divisional manager and the two regional managers; what a shock I got, as the interview was much harder than I had expected, and my nerves just got the better of me.

I swore that day I would never embarrass myself in an interview like that again. Halfway through the interview, I couldn't answer a question correctly, and that was the beginning of the end. It just got worse as time went on.

I really did consider getting up and leaving but knew if I did, my chances of ever becoming an area manager would be reduced drastically. I remember sitting in the car, crying, not because I didn't get the job, but because I had made a fool of myself and it would ruin it for future prospects. I then made it my mission to prove I was worthy of the role. These same three branches would go on to play such huge parts in my career years later.

In February of that year, I got a call from the Rom to inform me my manager was coming back, although I would stay in place until April, as he was on a phased return to work. I was disappointed, if I am honest. I was hoping he wouldn't come back. The branch was now performing, and we were working well as a team.

I was also grateful to be given the opportunity I had been given. Now I had to build on that and ensure all his hard work of teaching me didn't go to waste. He taught me how to plan and put strategies in place as well as instil accountability in others, while at the same time earning the respect from the team.

I also learned in my time as interim manager how to analyse and use data to keep making progress. Imagine all those years ago, the thought of these new skills I had developed over ten months would have sent me into shock.

Chapter 45

Life returned to normal, but I was now finding the role was as development manager was no longer enough to mentally challenge me. I was just really going through the motions.

I had only been back one month when another two area manager roles were advertised, this time for St Helens and Runcorn. Now, I was determined I was getting one of these branches and already decided if I was unsuccessful, it was time for me to move on. It was known within the company if you were rejected three times, you might as well give up. This was to be my third interview and probably the most difficult one after the last interview.

In between these two coming up, Manchester again came up, and if you were unsuccessful for them, then you were put forward for Manchester, so I really set my sights on Manchester. I didn't think I would get either of the other two.

I made sure I didn't make the mistake I had made in the previous interview. I did my homework to ensure there were no slip-ups.

I knew what my strengths were, and interviews were not one of them. I also knew once I got past that stage, I would be successful. Along with what the Rom had taught me as well as my own passion for winning, I knew what my own expectations were as a leader, if I was given the chance.

The day of the interview arrived. I drove to Sheffield. It was the same divisional manager as before, and the Rom for the newly opened region, as well as the deputy divisional manager. If I messed up this time, he certainly wouldn't have given me another chance.

The interview was set for the same day I was flying to Benidorm with Marie and friends. I had to go to Sheffield and be back within five hours, as I was leaving that afternoon. I did think about changing it, but thought otherwise, it may have looked like I wasn't serious.

Being a girl from Liverpool, we are known for fashion and spray tans, and the day before, I had decided to get one done. The worst possible thing happened: the tan went wrong, and my hands and feet were completely brown when I woke up on the day of the interview, and my face was orange.

I had a likeness to the character Madge off the programme *Benidorm*. Imagine the shock when I saw the damage. All I could think of was what would they think when I turned up like this. I tried everything from turps to bleach. I was determined to make a good impression. Now here I was, the palms of my hands a dirty brown. How was I ever going to get one of these jobs now?

I was devastated and thought, *Oh well, bang goes the job. I'll go anyway, and brown hands or not, I am going to give it my best shot.* I didn't know whether to laugh or cry and was dreading going into the interview room. As I walked in, the layout was completely different from the previous one, and straight away I felt comfortable, but I still had my hands to contend with. I also had to do a presentation, so my hands would be on full view. I thought my heart would come out of my chest, it was beating that fast.

My new potential boss was an Evertonian, and the two branches had been his. I had to really impress him with my stuff. I also decided (as much as it pained me to do it) to do all the covers for the presentation in blue (being a Red from Liverpool, that took a lot for me to do, but I also knew first impressions are what count).

As I went to shake their hands, I could see their faces. They probably wondered what I had done. Before they could say anything, I made a joke of it and said the first thing to come out of my mouth: 'Don't worry, it doesn't come off. I have tried everything'. Then all of sudden, I said, 'They are nothing compared to my feet'.

Why did I mention my feet? But it actually got a laugh, and then the divisional manager made a joke of how I would crack within thirty seconds. My reply to that was, 'Thanks for bigging me up, but it's usually twenty'.

That forged the rest of the interview; what I had thought would affect my chances actually helped me relax and think more clearly when answering questions. I was quite surprised at how articulate I was.

I left Sheffield on a high, knowing I had done enough. I got home with half an hour to spare, before meeting my sister and friends at the airport.

I was to call the regional manager the next day to find out if I was successful. That was the longest day and night waiting to make that call. I wanted a clear head the next morning, so I only had a couple of drinks. I didn't sleep a wink that night.

When I rang first thing the next morning, the phone went straight to voice mail. After more waiting for him to call me back, I didn't think my heart could take much more. When I saw his number come up, I didn't know whether to answer or not. This man was not just going to decide if I had a good holiday, but potentially my future and my dream job. Now it was crunch time. Marie and Lynn waited for a reaction. It was like a silent movie. As he was talking, I wasn't taking in what he was saying. I was pacing the floor, convinced because I was the only woman, I may not be successful.

I actually missed the bit where he congratulated me and just heard 'Runcorn' and thought, *Oh well, I wonder who got it,* and just as I was about to say thanks for letting me know, he said, 'So I am looking forward to working with you'.

Oh my goodness, I was the new area manager of Runcorn; what an accomplishment. I went to that interview thinking I may be good enough for Manchester South, now to find out I was first choice, I was ecstatic. I was finally going to live my dream. This was the start of my plan to one day not just run Liverpool as an interim manager, but to have my name above that door. My dream was now becoming reality, and that day in Benidorm, I knew I would do everything to achieve it.

Chapter 46

My first role as area manager started on 1 June 2009; that feeling I got when I saw my name on league tables attached to Runcorn is what always pushed me to get results. I was always uneasy if I wasn't green. I measured myself more than anyone needed to because of my competiveness, so the league tables played a major part in my successes.

I felt so proud of what I had achieved from leaving school, believing I would amount to nothing to now be responsible for a few million pounds turnover as well as leading a team of managers and agents. If only my parents and my old school teacher could see me now. This is what would motivate me, as well as motivating my team. I finished the year with a green contribution and in the top ten.

I was consistently improving, always coming up with new strategies to improve results. The knowledge I learned in the role, I always passed to my managers and agents, building competence in each and every one of them.

We regularly had promotions within the company, and as a branch, we were always in the top half of the tables. One time, I put in a competition based on Dragon's Den and named it Angela's Den; my managers were named after the Dragons. I had promised an agent I would wear an Everton top for a full day if he achieved his targets.

Well, he did hit his target, and as painful as it was to wear it, I did it. The competitions were always in good fun, and this was no different. My mum probably haunted me and called me a traitor.

I had the most wonderful mentor who taught me the job from an area manager's perspective, and it was his guidance and direction that started me on my path to success. I will always be grateful for the time and energy he put in to help me. I still consider him one of my closest friends today.

I will always look back at Runcorn with fond memories of where it all began for me. The friendly competitions between myself and my mentor are what would drive me forward and the laughs we had competing against each other, as well as the managers and agents, who always gave everything I asked of them. I had also put all my learnings my previous Rom had taught me into action, so I felt I was repaying his faith in me.

I also had a new Rom who had a different style of management from what I had been used to, but that same respect was as strong for him as it was for my previous Rom's. He was a very calm man who would influence me in a positive way. I could become quite irate when people try to kid me, but he taught me how to deal with this in a calm manner.

Change comes quite easily for me, so all the changes I made to my management style, I looked on as new skills. I was developing myself to grow as a leader.

I learned how to coach and develop skills within others, which would help them become more confident in their role, resulting in the location improving daily and my reputation getting stronger. This also helped my own confidence grow. I became bolder with what actions I took and plans I put in place.

Chapter 47

After eighteen months in Runcorn, my manager asked me would I consider moving to a bigger branch that would suit my skillset. He felt all that I had learned in Runcorn would put me in good stead for my new location, which had a different set of problems and was sitting at the bottom of the company. Although I was excited he had the faith in me to believe I was capable, I also had to weigh up the benefits of moving. More to the point, was I ready for such a big move?

I also had to speak with Barry and my boys first. I didn't want it affecting my home life. By now, Christopher had moved to London. He had not long got back from working in America for the summer and decided after enjoying the freedom of living abroad, Liverpool was no longer where he wanted to be.

I was devastated at the time but also proud of the confidence he displayed, making such a huge decision. He has now been in London for six years and has gone from strength to strength, ready to move into his own home with his girlfriend Gemma. My firstborn now ready to buy his first house makes my heart swell with so much pride. He displays that same work ethic and hunger to win as his mum. I know he along with Leighton and Joseph, he will always be successful, no matter what he puts his hand to.

I decided to take the promotion and manage Blackburn, a location with not just a much bigger debit, but also extra managers and agents to lead. The biggest achievement in my career has always been creating winners, and going to Blackburn just meant I was able to coach and develop more managers to exceed their own expectations.

In my mind, when I was first asked to go to Blackburn, I remember thinking of that day two years ago, when I was devastated at not getting that job, to now being asked would I think about it, as it needed a strong leader to turn it around. If I am honest, it felt good that they now realised their mistake in not appointing me initially, but it was probably the right decision at the time, as I was now more equipped to deal with the complexity of the branch.

I was excited and sad at the same time. I loved what the extra responsibility brought and getting my teeth into a new project, but I was sad at leaving Runcorn. I had not only recruited and trained two of the managers, I also oversaw the training of half the agency force, so I knew it was hard to walk away from here. They had also helped me build my reputation by taking on board what I was teaching them and running with it. I have always believed in empowering others if you are to get the best out of them, and this is what I had done with my team in Runcorn.

I was leaving a branch at the top of the division, earning regular bonuses, to go to one at the bottom and no bonus for the foreseeable future, but that didn't put me off. That just made me more determined to help these managers achieve bonus. Morale and team spirit were always lifted when a branch made bonus, so that became my focus.

I had to keep the news from the staff until after Christmas, as it could have affected results, and I didn't want them to lose their bonus they had worked so hard for. I felt such a fraud keeping this from them and felt like I was letting them down in some way. The staff and agents were so important to me. The respect I had for them was second to none. It was through their hard work and their belief in me that they worked so hard and the reason I was being offered a fantastic opportunity.

As soon as Christmas was over, I decided to tell them, although I wasn't supposed to. I felt I owed it to them to be honest. I have always shown my appreciation for hard workers and would often take them out as a thank you for their dedication, as well as showing my thanks over the years to the clerical staff. When bonus was made, they didn't receive any. They helped us, so I felt it only right that they should also benefit in some way. Not everyone was always happy that I would ask them to contribute a little to say thanks for their help, but I never once demanded they gave it. The choice was theirs, and if they said no, then I contributed more.

As well as being a supportive and encouraging manager, I also didn't suffer fools gladly, so as supportive as I was, I would also address issues immediately and challenge individuals if I thought they weren't contributing. That way, I would nip it in the bud straight away. Sometimes, the conversations I had with individuals would not be very nice; some took it on the chin and accepted it for what it was and also thanked me for the guidance and direction. It was so easy to lose your way and go off track, so sometimes these conversations were all that was needed. Others who were plain lazy and would try to do as little as possible felt it was personal, but that was never the case.

I was paid to do a job and would give everything I had, so I expected the same back, especially honesty and trust. If someone betrayed that trust, I dealt with it accordingly.

I managed others in the same manner have always liked to be managed: with respect, integrity, and trust, and if I hadn't done my duties, I held my hands up, apologised, and moved on, so I expected the same from my staff. If they were honest with me, I respected that in them and would go out of my way to support and guide them. Lazy and dishonesty didn't go down well, though, and the conversation would be a very different one.

If every person plays their part and conducts their duties to the best of their ability, then this creates a happy working environment, and they feel valued.

When I first arrived in a new branch, I would observe the people and find out their attitudes towards the job and what their aspirations were. Whenever anyone told me they wanted to progress, it was like music to my ears. My greatest pleasure as a leader was to help others achieve their goal. Although I didn't suffer fools, I was also very good at building relationships with others.

I believe this came from growing up with six best friends. From an early age, forging relationships and being a people person came naturally, so these skills were always what saw me through.

I sat my staff down to tell them the news. This was harder than I thought it would be. We had come so far in eighteen months, and the bond I had with each of them, as well as the agents, made the decision to leave harder. I grew as a person every day I was there, with the different obstacles I faced, but I also knew for me to keep growing, I had to grab this opportunity with both hands.

Chapter 48

I started in Blackburn on 1 February 2011, just twenty months after first being promoted to area manager. My determination to succeed in this branch was based on a number of factors, firstly to prove to myself I was worthy of this promotion and secondly to demonstrate why they should have appointed me as the area manager two years ago. That alone made my desire to succeed even more important.

I knew I had my hands full. To me, it was just a bigger version of what I had left behind. The only difference, it had been at the bottom of the company for the last two years, and that made it all the more appealing to me. Turning this branch around would definitely be a feather in my cap. I also had great support in the Rom and H/R manager, so I knew there wasn't room for failure.

As previously, I didn't go in there judging what I had heard. People are quite often influenced by others' opinions. Because I am so strong minded, I have never allowed someone else's judgement to define what I thought of a person. I made my own mind up about them.

I observed as well as listened to the conversations the managers were having with the agents and how they were getting the message out. Positive and inspirational attitudes were what I believed made great managers.

I had six managers, one woman and five men; although I get on well with both sexes, I tend to get along more with women. Maybe this comes from my childhood. This woman would go on to not just be a great manager but also a friend who I trusted completely. Watching her grow from when I first started to when I left was breath-taking.

Two weeks after my arrival, the H/R manager came in to join me in having one-to-ones with each of the managers. In addition to observing the behaviour within the management force, I analysed trends and data, sometimes until three in the morning, looking for ways to improve results and what the issues were. In the business I was in, there were quick fixes, but I was never comfortable with this and looked long term, so would work through until I came up with a solution.

I wanted to get to know them individually before working together as a team. I wanted to know what made them tick and also to reassure them I wasn't the Cruella De Ville they were expecting. I was actually a very approachable person who was willing to support and coach them in their quest to grow. Sometimes, my reputation went before me because of how I dealt with underperformance. I also wanted to get the message across quite clearly without scaremongering. I would not tolerate excuses.

If an individual displayed a good work ethic and results were still not coming in, I had every sympathy for them and would do everything in my power to help them along.

I wasn't naïve enough to believe improvements happened overnight, so I knew this was for the long term. We all had to get used to how each other worked and what we had to do to progress as a branch. I also knew when you put your heart and soul into a project, then success follows.

In every location I worked, training brought the biggest improvements. From an agent through to area manager, I always made sure when I trained an individual, they were trained to the highest level. If I wanted results from them, then they had to be fully equipped to get them.

I ensured my agents were competent in their abilities to earn top rate commission. I had seen first-hand the difference a great mentor can make. I was more productive in my role, due to how I had been trained from my first role as interim manager in Liverpool to my position in Runcorn, and results would come fast.

Also, when an agent is trained well and they start increasing their commission, their respect is tenfold, and they will go over and beyond for you. My passion has always been in coaching and mentoring, and that is where I first wanted to become a coach.

The support and development of agents decided what results came in. It was important that communication was always high on the agenda, right across the board.

That meeting attended by the H/R manager with each staff member was probably the most valuable lesson I ever had in my career. As well as me getting to know the managers, the H/R manager was also observing me and gave feedback on everything that had happened in my office, not just how the managers were answering questions, but also how I was asking them.

Weaknesses and self-awareness are not something we like to admit to or like to think about, but we all have them, and mine had come out on that day. I could come across as abrupt; it is my worst trait. Also, tolerance had reared its ugly head once again, so I knew this was something I really had to work on.

I have always taken constructive criticism well, and today was no different. He had taught me, as he had done over the years, how to treat people, and this is what made him a fantastic H/R manager. The way in which he delivered his findings was such that I was also learning and the same time teaching others.

Chapter 49

In March of that year, I was invited on a winner's day out to Aintree Racecourse. I will never forget the conversation between myself and the divisional manager. He advised me he thought I would fail; he told me Blackburn was a big battle and asked if I thought I was strong enough.

I simply answered, 'Yes'.

His reply was, 'I don't think you are'.

By now I was getting annoyed at what he was saying, as I walked away, I just informed him I don't lose battles. Inside, I was laughing. He didn't know me as a person nor what I had already overcome nor how ambitious I was.

I also understood his concerns; he needed to know I was in this for the long haul. Being the worst branch, it would have been difficult for even the most experienced manager to turn around.

I also knew he had to approve the move I made to Blackburn, so he must have had some faith in me. He was just testing me and my desire to succeed.

I guaranteed him Blackburn would rise from the ashes and we would be talking about it for very different reasons the following year. He gave a little laugh at my reaction. We shook hands and left it that.

Over time, results were slowly coming in, and there were snippets of improvements here and there. Morale was lifting and spirits were high. On my arrival, these managers were so deflated by what they were known as, I wanted to prove to them and every single person who had called them. They were good people who had lacked direction and guidance of how to work together as a team; also, they were not given the credit they deserved.

After a few months working with them, I found the majority were willing, able, and wanting to come on the journey of putting Blackburn back where it should be. They just needed someone to believe in them so they could believe in themselves.

When you work in big organisations, there will always be decisions you are not comfortable making, and as much as I knew the effect it had on individuals, I also knew they had to be made, no matter how bad I felt.

I have always believed if you have done everything to help someone and you find you have come to the end of the road with them, the decision is made for you. There are people who are not capable of change, and there are others who just don't want to change, but even though they made the decisions by the actions they took, I still found it hard to be put in that position.

This was the only part of the job I disliked; disciplining people was something I wasn't comfortable with. I got more out of praising them, contrary to what people thought of me. Due to the fact I dealt with laziness and underperformers, I was seen as having a heart of stone. If only they knew how some of those decisions stopped me sleeping at night.

I knew it would affect their whole future, but I had to separate myself from this. I had a job I was being paid well for. I was expected to be the person others saw me as.

All the hard work from the agents, managers, and myself paid off: We were getting a visit from the field director.

This had never happened before. This really was to be celebrated. We had come so far in five months. We had also got bonus for the first time in three years in the July. Now, we were on a high, and my biggest reward was seeing the smiles on their faces.

The foundations were now laid, the platform ready to be built. Blackburn really was coming alive, and my managers and agents were doing the job others were convinced they couldn't do.

Although the wheels were now turning, I don't know how many times I questioned my decision to move.

I would look at Runcorn; all my hard work was benefitting someone else, and here I was, working silly hours with nothing to show for it, only tired eyes and higher mileage on my car, for the ninety-six miles I was travelling to get me to and from the office. In all of that time, I never once thought of quitting. If I give my word, I made it my business to follow it through. Conquering Blackburn was something I was determined to do. If I was having a difficult day, I would draw on my parents' strength and how they overcame adversity, faced with the prospect of no money to feed your children. My situation was never as bad as that, so this really was a walk in the park for me.

The day of reckoning arrived, and the director arrived. The office was buzzing. We were so excited to get this visit.

This meant the branch was now being spoken about for different reasons, just as I had predicted to the divisional manager.

On his arrival, the mood amongst the staff was shining through. My I/C and I were there to greet him. I remember him telling me Rome wasn't built in a day, and my I/C replied, 'Yes, but Angie wasn't the foreman'.

He thought I was being too optimistic when I told him the branch would finish the year green. That was the wonderful thing about taking on Blackburn. They were giving me the time to turn it around. It had been performing so badly, there was no expectation.

That visit from the field director made me even more determined to prove how strong my managers and agents were.

We did finish with a green contribution and within the top ten of the league. That for me was the greatest accolade my staff and agents could have given me. If I am honest, I was being overly optimistic, but when I set myself goals, nothing can stand in my way.

Over the months, I kept surprising myself at the milestones we were reaching as a branch, and as we would reach one, I would then set our sights even higher. By the end of the year, we were the only branch (out of a total of twenty-eight) to hit a target the company had put in place. This meant the biggest bonus my managers had ever had at once. That was like winning an Oscar. I remember ringing the divisional manager and laughing with him, advising him the battle was now won. He told me he had no doubt I would succeed.

Ten months after that all-important visit, I got a phone call from the field director, inviting me to have lunch with a number of other area managers, himself, and the director of the company. My goodness, now imagine my parents if they could see me, sitting around the boardroom table, discussing tactics on how to make improvements. My opinion was what they wanted, along with those of the other area managers. They were interested in what we do to be successful and what strategies we put in place.

As nervous as I was about attending that meeting, I knew once I was there, I could hold my own. I have so much self-belief. This was instilled in me from that tiny little girl in Radcliffe Walk.

When I first got that call, I thought it was someone joking around; why would he ring me out of over two hundred managers? I have always been the same. Although I know my own capabilities, I find it hard that others can actually see it. That phone call knocked me for six. When I did realise it was him, I suddenly became tongue-tied and couldn't even form a sentence.

I believe that was their way of saying thank you for all the work I had put in both branches. The first person I wanted to tell was Barry. I would never have achieved any of my successes without his support; even bad days were turned into good ones. When I arrived home after a long day, he did anything he could to take away the pressure of the job.

Yes, I was invited to lunch with the directors for the work I had done, but this was also the work of my wonderful team that had given me so much support since my arrival. It wasn't easy for them getting used to a new manager, and me being a perfectionist was even harder for them to adapt to, but they also knew the changes we were making would benefit them also. By instilling confidence in others, they would then go to on to thrive.

In all of my achievements I had in my career, watching my manager in Blackburn tell me she wasn't looking to progress, to actually be appointed as the area manager of Blackburn less than two years later, I was proud of how far she had come. Everything I had taught her was now paying off. The pride I felt at her appointment was better than anything I had achieved before.

Chapter 50

I had only been at Blackburn for sixteen months, and the same thing happened. My manager asked me to look after Bolton for one month whilst the manager was off ill, again another branch I was unsuccessful for three years before; this was now becoming a joke. This would be the second time in just over a year I was being asked to oversee another underperforming branch. By now, I was starting to feel resentful. I was becoming a victim of my own success. Yes, I was willing to support the division as well as the region, but I wasn't being given the time to enjoy my hard work. As I would start relaxing and enjoy the role, they would ask me to take on another branch.

As usual, I did not make a decision until I spoke with Barry, and again, he would tell me to do what I was happy with.

I arrived in Bolton on 1 July 2012 for what should have been a month; it turned into nearly three. Even though I was feeling resentful, I looked at it as adding more strings to my bow.

I went into that branch with the same methods I had always used. As well as observing and listening, I would upskill, encourage, and support them. Some of the branches I managed were harder than others, and some of the staff didn't always comply with the changes. This would be the biggest problem to get people on your side. More often than not, I did, but those who were lazy wouldn't be happy when they saw me walk through the door. They knew there was no place to hide.

Bolton was completely different from the previous three branches I had managed. It is in Greater Manchester, and the rivalry between the two teams is high. As I walked into the area manager's office, the first thing I noticed was a picture of Sir Alex Ferguson and the Manchester United team on the wall. It was one thing taking me from my own branch, but if anyone thought I would sit and look at this picture for the next month, they had another thing coming. My mum would turn in her grave if I hadn't taken that picture down.

As the day went on, I had to come up with a plan that wouldn't offend the managers. If I wanted these people on my side, I didn't want to come across as bitter, so I had to be very shrewd without insulting their intelligence. As much as I disliked Man United, Alex Ferguson was a genius when it came to football, so I sat there thinking, *How would he play this one?*

I walked over, took the photo down, and placed it with their faces to the wall; at the time, I remember thinking, *They won't buy what I am about to say.*

So I made them a cup of tea and called them into the office. There were three men and one woman whom was on holiday, and all of them United supporters, to make it even worse.

'Why is the picture down?' one of them asked.

I started with, 'Right, guys, United are your team, just like mine are Liverpool'. Although Liverpool were struggling at the time, they were very successful when I was growing up, first with Bob Paisley and then along came Kenny Dalglish. Man United were the team to beat right now.

I just went straight into it and asked, 'Why do you think they have been so successful?'

They all looked at me as if I had two heads; one of them answered, 'Because we have the best manager'.

They weren't expecting the answer I gave, coming from a Liverpool supporter. 'Well, they weren't, until Sir Alex arrived'.

I added, 'He had to build a team from scratch and is now rated as one of the best in the world; that keeps happening because they all pull together and work together as teams should'. They were still looking at me, wondering where the conversation was going. 'You don't get that if you have a player out of position'.

I have always looked at my role as similar to a football manager; you play the team to their strengths, and you work on what needs improving. You then put them in the position that brings the biggest success. When I explained this to them, they did not so much as agree with me but could see the logic of where I was coming from.

No one, no matter what job you have or what position you are in, no one enjoys being at the bottom, and these managers were no different.

I told them when we started working as a team, I would turn the picture around, and when we started meeting objectives consistently, I would then put it back in its place. If I am honest, I was hoping I would be gone before that happened.

Again as before, team spirit was the major factor, along with direction, and without blowing my own trumpet, I find this comes naturally to me. When you empower people, you are immediately creating a positive atmosphere. If individuals feel valued, they will take that extra step for you.

No matter what the situation, I always have a positive attitude and an enthusiastic outlook. This in itself always worked for me. Again, this came from my childhood. The eight of us were a team, and we could do anything as long as we were one. I have carried this right throughout my life.

As weeks went on and the team became stronger, I would turn the picture around, reminding them of what we working towards.

July saw small improvements but not enough to make bonus or put the picture back up. In August, we finished with a green contribution and bonus in the bag, and the picture went back on the wall (although for the rest of the time I was there, I did my best to avoid looking at it).

In every branch I worked in, I learnt a new skill, and Bolton was where I came into my own when it came to influencing others.

I returned to Blackburn on 22 September after overseeing both branches; because I was concentrating on Bolton, Blackburn was struggling and had gone down in the league table. My I/C had done a fantastic job, but this was a volatile location, and she was only just starting on her journey. It was always going to be difficult for her.

The relief I felt when I walked through that door to a hot cup of tea on my desk, I felt like I was going home; of all the branches I have worked, from agent through to area management, this was the branch I held closest to my heart. It had been written off for a long time, and we had proven you should never write anything off. We proved anything can be done if you are passionate about it.

Every person played their part in the success of this branch, from the agents and managers through to the clerical team and the cleaner, ensuring there was a warm drink to greet you when you arrived.

Chapter 51

Here I was, back in Blackburn with a new divisional manager. I had been back for just over a week when he came in to visit and introduce himself. As the ones before him, he came with the same question: Would I consider a move to Manchester?

I told him I wasn't interested in any more moves for at least twelve months. I wanted to carry on where I had left off in June. I had set myself a new goal: I wanted to take Blackburn to number one in the company, so I had no intention of moving anywhere. I also craved stability. As soon as I got comfortable somewhere, I felt as though they were already getting my next branch ready for me.

I was also physically and mentally drained, not just from the work that had to go into turning theses branches, but also the decisions I had to make on some people were not good ones. I started to dislike the person I was being turned into.

I had originally gone into management to help and inspire people to achieve the ultimate. Now, I felt like I was doing the opposite.

Again I felt I was being used in some way, so I wasn't happy that every time I got a branch performing again, it would be taken away from me and someone else would reap the rewards. I made my mind up that day, I was going to think about a new career.

Just before going to Bolton, I had attended a company conference in Bradford, which was presented by a man who influenced my decision two years later in my chosen career.

I was just another attendee in the crowd that day but felt drawn to this man. What he was doing was very similar to what I was doing in branches. I was there to build and motivate teams to get results, and this is what this man was doing, just on a much bigger scale. I remember being mesmerised by the way he captivated the audience that day and how he inspired me by just listening to him.

This man had awakened something inside me to research how I could become a motivational speaker and coach. From that day, I wanted to reach out to more people than I had ever done before.

The divisional manager left the office, and I was thinking he accepted what I had said.

I just wanted to be left alone to do my job. After being back around seven weeks, the branch had climbed back up to ninth place in the league, so my sights on number one were getting closer.

On 7 November, the regional manager arrived unannounced, which was unusual, and then when the divisional manager turned up, I knew what was coming.

He again asked me if I would consider moving to Manchester South. This was becoming a bit of a joke now. I had been turned down for all three branches nearly four years before, but now everyone of them needed my expertise. I felt like all I was ever going to be was a trouble-shooter who would be used every time a branch was struggling. I was now so fed up that I considered leaving, but I knew the time wasn't right.

Although I was angry and upset, I also knew there was no point arguing, so I decided I would take up the offer of Manchester. As soon as the time was right, I would move to new pastures.

The one thing I was happy for was that my manager was appointed to area manager when I left. She so deserved this job after the journey she had been on from my first day with her.

Chapter 52

I arrived in Manchester on 14 November 2012. By now, my passion for the job was gone, and the energy I had always displayed was also gone. I was losing my sparkle as well as the smile that was always painted on my face. Even that difficult day I had spent with my mum I smiled, although I was broken inside, so it said everything that it was now disappearing.

I had done the same thing so many times. It no longer gave me that buzz inside when I got results. If I am honest, by the time I got to this branch, I was already switched off and thinking about a new career.

After being in Manchester for three months and all the hours stuck on the motorway, I decided I was now going to ask for a move instead of the other way around. The branch was really struggling, and I had become so bored of going through the motions of motivating some to having strong conversations with others. I was no longer interested in the job. A branch in Liverpool had come up, and after being denied it the first time, I was finally invited to a meeting with the regional manager.

I just wanted to get the job done and go home, so a branch closer to home was perfect for me. After arriving at his office not knowing what he was going to tell me, he informed me I would be taking over the newly named

Knowsley branch, at the bottom of the company. This didn't put me off at all. I felt now I was home, I could take my time turning it around. I walked out of that office so grateful for what I had just been told. I promised the regional manager that I wouldn't let him down.

I arrived in Knowsley on 3 April 2013. I only worked under his leadership for just over three months, but I learned so much from him and how to apply my qualities in a positive way to get results.

I didn't let him down. I took this branch from the bottom of the company to number one in eight weeks. I had achieved the ultimate; I also had the top three managers out of a company total of over a thousand. Wow, how had I done this so quickly? I knew my sparkle was coming back, but this was in a league of its own. Not even I could have predicted this.

As before, first and foremost, these managers were jumping from one task to another, not knowing what direction to go in as well as working individually, so again, this is where I started before moving on to the capabilities of the staff. Although this result was fantastic, I felt it was in the wrong branch. I had wanted this so much for my team in Blackburn; the managers in Knowsley were completely different from what I had been used to. You would think when a branch was sitting at number one, the smiles would be there for the world to see, but that didn't happen here. The reaction was surreal for me. I didn't connect with any of these managers at all. Attitudes and willingness make a whole lot of difference to a branch. Not even the possibility of bonuses could put a smile on their faces. That's when I decided it was definitely time to move on.

Eight weeks after my arrival, we were called to a meeting with the Rom. Although there had been rumours of redundancies, it had not been confirmed until now. I knew I was ready for a change, but there was something about redundancy. I felt it was just another word for dismissal, just on a larger scale. I had always wanted to go when I decided, not when someone else did.

That not knowing went on for another three weeks before I found out I was okay; they had worked it on a matrix, and I was in a pot with two other area managers. I kissed the Rom with sheer relief that I was okay.

Looking back now, it probably would have been the right decision for me. Not long after, I ended up going off on long-term sick. My body had finally had enough. I was by now a shadow of my former self. My health was suffering due to all the upheaval in the last few years as well as from the threat of redundancy. The emotional effect the job had on me had finally taken its toll. At one point, my doctor wanted to admit me to hospital.

In the time I was off work, my friend Mandy died. I had met her through my friends Paula and Sandra; this news completely devastated all of us, and her death then made me question my own future. She had died very suddenly and left a young daughter. I knew then I had to really think about my own health. What I was going through wasn't just affecting me but also Barry and my boys.

After being off a couple of months, I decided I would go back in September. On my return, there had been another reshuffle. I now found myself responsible for the newly formed South Mersey. Two of the top sections I had in Knowsley had now been transferred to St Helens and were replaced with the bottom three of South Liverpool.

This was now becoming normal practise – me being responsible for upskilling individuals on a regular basis, no one really taking into account the emotional aspect of what I was expected to do.

Right now, I didn't know whether I was excited because I had finally reached my long-term goal of running this branch, seventeen years after standing in that office and promising myself I would have my name above the door. All that I had worked for was right in front of me.

I had only been back six weeks and found myself off ill again; this is because I wasn't well enough when I went back in September. If ever I was on the edge, it was now. Instead of being admitted to hospital, I had to agree to counselling from my doctor.

This was caused through working myself to the bone. And all for what? To now have to start again. This had been going on now for over four years. I felt my sanity and health were never taken into account when the decisions were made to move me from branch to branch. I have also learned so much over the years and developed skills that would serve me right through life.

On my return in November, I was transferred to Leigh until after Christmas; this was to help me back on a phased return. When I did go back, I knew my time really was coming to an end.

I moved back to South Mersey on 2 January, determined to go out with a bang, and finished the first quarter second in the region to a man I had always looked up to. Over the years, if I was close to him in the league tables, I knew I was doing well, so to be second to him would have normally thrilled me.

The second quarter started, and I was becoming increasingly unhappy in my role. I knew I had to make a decision. Integrity had always played a major part in my life, so I felt like I was being untrue to myself and the company by not giving my all to the role. Also, there was nothing left for me to achieve. I had already decided what I wanted to do, and being part of the company was not in my plan for the future. Promotion didn't even interest me. I believed I had more to offer.

April came and went, and I was getting ready for my annual holiday with the girls. Our yearly jaunt to Benidorm would normally have me all excited, but not even that could lift my mood. I knew what I had to do, but I kept thinking, *Just go on holiday and see how I feel on my return* (as in my mind, I still wasn't sure what I needed to do to become a coach). If I did leave, what would I do? This job had been my life for so long. It was hard to imagine not gearing myself up for a day, not getting excited at the thought of getting results.

Chapter 53

A week before I was due to go away, I decided to resign. I woke up full of excitement. I knew this was the first day of the rest of my life: No more fifteen-hour days, no more sleepless nights, and no more feeling bad due to decisions I had to make. I was now ready for a new chapter to begin.

All those years ago when I dreamt of being a manager and running South Liverpool, now here I was about to throw it all away. Why? Because I knew my own capabilities and knew I was ready to be a new me.

I had told Barry that morning what I was about to do. Just like before, his support would be there once again. He told me whatever I chose to do, he would be behind me all the way.

I have never questioned his loyalty, and a lot of the decisions I have made would have been much harder without his support. He could also see the signs that were there the year before.

I was becoming ill again; because of the damage it had done the year before, he did not want me to go back to that person.

I had been under the doctor for nearly two years now, and before that, I may have visited twice a year. After the events of the year before, I was not prepared to go down that path again. I believe when something no longer serves you as a person, you should move on, not just for yourself but also for the company. It would have been unfair of me to stay. This job was no longer giving me that buzz I had for all those years, so I owed it to the company to leave.

I had always prided myself on giving 100 percent in my role, and if I was no longer prepared for that, it was unfair to carry on (although I was walking away from security and still not sure what to do).

I went into work as normal on the busiest day of the week for us as a company. We had the agents in for interview day. Some of these agents I had managed years ago, as well as when I was the interim area manager. I would miss them dearly, along with some of the managers. Like everything, you have different relationships with people. In South Mersey, I had one manager who brightened my day up every day. She had been through so much herself and always had a smile on her face, so I would miss that smile that greeted me every day.

By noon that day, I had verbally resigned. My manager at the time asked me to put it in writing (he obviously thought I would change my mind). It was a bold decision to quit that day, and a lot of people would have changed their mind by the time it came to putting it in writing, but once I have made my mind up, there is no changing it. Twenty years ago, I just decided to quit smoking because I didn't want my children growing up around it. I have never smoked since; when my mind is made up, I don't often change it.

By five o'clock that day, I had put it in writing, and that night was the first time I had slept properly in two years. That is when I knew I had made the right decision; my mind was at peace. Although I did wonder if everything would work out, those doubts didn't last long. I thought back to all the other decisions I had made, and that put my mind at ease.

By the beginning of June, I couldn't muster up the energy much longer and actually went off sick. I often questioned myself on how I could have gone from loving my job so much that I would skip into work and sometimes not even realise it was so late when I would be leaving, to actually watching the clock until five o'clock came and I could go home. I had thrived on working these hours in Runcorn and Blackburn. Now I couldn't even work an eight-hour day.

Chapter 54

Over the weeks after I resigned, I researched motivational speakers and found the ones everyone had heard of (Tony Robbins, Les Brown and Brian Tracey), but I also came across a guy called Brendon Burchard. Now, he just seemed to resonate with me and made me want it even more. I also wanted to find the old me again. Up until two years before, I turned every difficult situation around with humour, and now I had to reclaim that person, so I also decided to research comedy courses.

I found a course with the Liverpool Comedy Festival; a guy called Sam Avery was the tutor. The fee of £120 was to be the best money I ever spent.

I arrived for the six-week course in the Radio City Tower. This was called the Tower Restaurant when I was growing up. I had my first date in here with Barry and my friend Debbie, who passed away nine years ago (she was also Tracey's aunty), so this held very special memories for me.

I always regret that I hadn't seen her for a couple of years before she died. Along with Debbie and Tracey, their family had meant so much to me growing up. They lived in Bebbington when were kids, and Tracey and I would stay over in the summer. That is when I first met Debbie; she was a couple of years older than me.

When I was fourteen, I remember my first drink in a bar on the Wirral, wearing her clothes and make-up because I had sneaked out. I remember thinking how grown-up I felt, trying to walk in my three-inch heels with my clutch bag under my arm. I couldn't even go to the bar, I was that small and looked even younger than I was.

Here I was, now, about to go to the top of the Tower; it would bring bittersweet memories for me. Thinking back, I could still see Debbie's face, laughing at how excited I was on my first date, and then I shed a tear for Debbie and her passing away so young, leaving two beautiful children behind.

It was times like this that made me more determined to be happy as well as try to give something back; life is so precious, and it can be gone in the blink of an eye. We are happier when are giving and helping, and that's the reason my chosen career would be coaching. I know I have got so much to give others and help them towards reaching their goals.

I still wasn't sure if I ever wanted to work back in the corporate world. This had been my life for so long, but what I did know is I needed time away from it. I always think you should step out of your comfort zone now and again and do something random.

As I sat around in a line of five men and myself, Sam talking us through the course, my mind was everywhere, wondering what in God's name made me think I could do this, when he informed us we had to stand up and speak for 30 seconds, talking about anything that came to our mind. I nearly collapsed; oh my goodness, my whole body went into spasm. I was shaking at the thought of it. I thought, *I'll go last, we may run out of time.* Wishful thinking.

I got up and started with the most random thing and talked about wearing pink socks, having them all look down at my feet, even though I didn't have any socks on. They still all looked down, giving me time to think of something else to say; my mind was just blank. My mouth was dry, and I was looking at Sam to call time. That was the longest thirty seconds of my life. It's not very often I am lost for words, but I was that night. I even questioned whether I would go back the following week.

After the two hours in there and getting the feel for being on stage, realising we were all just as nervous as each other, and we all had our reasons for being there, I went out of there, just like I had done when I worked in Blackburn, with a spring in my step.

I realised how much I had lost in the last two years. I hadn't smiled from my heart or soul in all that time, and it was only today that made me recognise that my smile had always been my logo and now it was back. As we were just about to leave, Sam told us to think of a subject we could work on; the final week, we would be putting a gig on for family and friends. This had to be seven minutes long; now I had palpitations.

I couldn't even do thirty seconds, so how in God's name would I get through seven minutes? That was a lifetime, but as with everything else, I took it in my stride and thought, *Well, I have started this now, so I have to finish it.*

Over the weeks, Barry helped me work on the material. I practised at every opportunity, recording my voice and going over and over it. The sound of my own voice was making me worse. As always, Barry and my boys helped me. They were my biggest critics and told me what to add and what to take out.

When I told people what I was doing, they thought I had lost the plot. One friend said I was having a midlife crisis. It may have looked this way to others, but I had decided two years before that I wanted to be different and do what made me happy. I had worked by somebody else's rules and regulations my whole life. Now, I had decided it was time for me to own my life and decide my own future.

So here I was, five weeks after that first night in the Tower, at the Baby Blue in the Albert Dock, ready to go on stage in front of two hundred friends and family. I still hadn't perfected my routine and felt sick inside.

On our way to the venue, I told Barry to turn the car around, I couldn't do it; as usual, he was telling me I would be fine and I had family and friends attending, so I had to go. He added that I inspired him by how brave I was. Those words from the man I look to for support were all I needed to carry on.

The show started at seven; we had to arrive at six to practise and get used to the stage. My heart was beating so fast, I thought it would go into shock and stop. All the families and friends were arriving. I was pacing the floor, thinking to myself, *What have I done? I am going to embarrass myself, as well as my friends and family*. My mentor from my previous job was sitting in the crowd. I was praying to my mum and dad to help me through the gig. Dad would have been looking down, saying, 'There she goes again, going against the norm', and my mum would be telling everyone I was a comedian.

All I could think of was how six weeks ago, I couldn't do thirty seconds; how was I getting through this? The first guy went on, and his routine seemed to be over before it started.

I was standing at the back of the room when Sam called my name. As I walked up, I could see Barry's back to me. I rubbed it to give me the courage to get up there. I knew no matter how good or bad I was, he would be there to hold me at the end. Going on that stage with two hundred pairs of eyes staring back at me, I felt like a rabbit trapped in headlights.

When I started off, I couldn't form a sentence without my voice faltering, but in that crowd, I could see Barry's face and him saying, 'You can do it', and then I was in free flow and could not believe where it had come from. Now I was getting the laughs, and my confidence was growing.

When I was on that stage, I thought of my mum and all she missed out on and how funny she was. When I meet people who knew her, they all speak of her with a tale and a smile and how much she made them laugh. If I had done the same on that night, then I had achieved more than I could ever have imagined.

Being compared to her as a mum is a massive compliment, but to be told I also had her character: that was like winning the lottery for me. She had been my first friend, my inspiration, my anchor, and my role model right throughout my life. No matter what life threw her way, she came out of it with that beautiful smile that would so often light up her face. Now here I was, eleven years after losing her, replaying that day in my memory, thinking I will never smile again, but somehow, I was not just smiling but making a crowd of two hundred smile too.

When I came off the stage, it was to a big round of applause. I could only have dreamt about that. I asked

Barry how long it went on for, and he told me nearly ten minutes. Wow, six weeks ago, I couldn't even do thirty seconds, now I had surpassed all my own expectations.

Two weeks after the gig, my husband was in a supermarket when he overheard a reporter asking the checkout lady if there were any local stories to place in the *Anfield and Walton Star*. Barry told him about my gig and how I had over two hundred hits in the first two weeks on YouTube. The reporter then asked if he could interview me about the gig.

This story was published the week after. My gig was then posted on Twitter and retweeted by Jim Davidson, John Aldridge, and more importantly Ronnie Whelan (this man was my schoolgirl crush and now he has not just watched my gig but also retweeted it); who would have thought? Only months before, I was on the brink of depression and a breakdown. That course I nearly never finished saved me and gave me back my life.

Link to my gig, feel free to watch. https://m.youtube.com/watch?v=inmqKHF7xN4

Chapter 55

That six-week course was a turning point in my life. I now knew I wanted to make people smile, but I also knew it wasn't as a comedian. It felt so right being on that stage. Motivational speaking and inspiring others to believe was all I was thinking about.

If I could help people become the best version of themselves, then I would be giving something back.

I believe we are put on this earth for a purpose, and when you find your own purpose, that is when you truly start living.

I always knew I was at my happiest when I was helping others, whether that was saving my mum money as a child to buy food or helping my children to get a good education. I now realised this was my vocation in life.

I was born a people person, and this is where my passion lay. I also love talking. If I put all of this together, I know I can benefit others.

After I had finished the course, I was determined to carry on searching for ways to achieve my dream. I came across a two-day taster course with the Coaching Academy. When I attended this course, I knew as soon as I walked in that this was for me. I had found me, and that's when my dream started to become a reality.

Over the two days, we covered the concept of coaching and what it represented, the dimensions of it, and most importantly, how it can help people. We also went through the different models of coaching, from corporate, small businesses, health, and wellbeing to youth and parent impact.

Although I have loved my time working in business and the successes I achieved, as soon as I heard the words 'parent and youth', I got the strangest feeling. My vocation was staring me in the face. They say when that happens, doors open on their own, and that is exactly what took place.

My biggest success in my life has been my children.

I believe this the hardest but most rewarding job in the world. Whatever I taught my children as a parent and teacher would either make or break them as adults, and

I made it my priority to always inspire them to be the best they could ever be.

My boys are now men, and I believe my journey is just beginning.

My dream is to eventually go to India and make a difference. This comes from a documentary I watched on the street children of Mumbai. Even if it is to help one child, I believe I will have given back for the privileges I never in a million years thought I would have when I was a child.

I am now partway through my diploma into coaching and know from experience how difficult it is to grow up with nothing but love and hope, as well as a dream. I also know how important it is to set yourself a goal and believe. If you have someone there who believes in you and pushes you, then you can become anything, and that is why I have chosen this path.

I would like to help as many parents instil that same work ethic in their children that was instilled in me all those years ago, as well as that hunger to win. Growing up in a family of eight with so little, yet still able to laugh and be grateful for being born, is what started my road to being who I am today.

In my next step in my quest to become a motivational speaker, I attended a two-day event in London and stood on the stage talking in front of over 150 people about my goal to work with and help as many children and parents as possible.

I met so many fantastic people on that course who want to make a difference to others. From there, I then attended another event with the Public Speaking Academy to boost my confidence when talking on stage. I believe the biggest investment you can make is in yourself, and I will continue to do this even when I have realised my dream and become a motivational speaker.

If someone would have told me all those years ago what I would have achieved, through all the heartaches, trials, and tribulations, I wouldn't have believed them.

Our children of today are the future of tomorrow, and that is why I am so passionate when it comes to them. I want as many parents and children to experience what I and my children have achieved, as well as always reach for the stars.

I have now set myself a new goal along with motivational speaking. It is important to keep as many doors open to enhance our growth as individuals.

If you have read this book, that means it has got past my biggest critics, my husband and sons as well as being my constant support through everything. They are also very honest with their words.

And in the words of Gerry Marsden, 'You'll never walk alone'.

Printed in Great Britain
by Amazon.co.uk, Ltd.,
Marston Gate.